AF265219

# The Cannabis Papers

# The Cannabis Papers

*A citizen's guide to cannabinoids*

*By Publius*

© 2011 Creative Commons 3.0

ISBN: 978-0-615-17241-5

Made in the United States of America.

_This book is dedicated to beginnings._

*The Drug War has gone too far.*

*Sitting in your Ivory Towers*
*Making laws against the flowers*
*While flowers of choice, your choice, are fine.*
*Coffee, cigarettes and wine,*
*State Supported*
*State Promoted*
*Advertised and Subsidized.*
*With wiretaps and pre-dawn busts,*
*Your Pot Commandos power lusts,*
*Make the cartels rich as nations,*
*While you pass your legislation,*
*Designed for sound bite spin gyrations.*
*You burn their crops.*
*You corrupt their cops.*
*You drive prices to their tops.*
*Spending billions.*
*Watching millions.*
*Confiscate a home, a car,*
*Bend over search,*
*Piss in the jar.*
*Supply-demand and rising prices,*
*Paid in blood and sexual vices.*
*They cope with dope*
*But it's you that pays,*
*With midnight fears of alleyways.*
*You're both torching pipes and laying lines,*
*Who'll be first to change their minds?*

*The Drug War has gone too far.*

by Morgyn

# Table of Contents

<u>*The crow and the pitcher*</u>

*For weeks and weeks there had been no rain. The streams and pools had dried to dust, and all of the animals were thirsty. Two crows, flying together in search of water, spotted a pitcher that had been left on a garden wall. They flew to it and saw that it was half full of water. But neither one could reach far enough inside the pitcher's narrow neck to get a drink.*

*"There must be a way to get that water," said the first crow. "If we think it through, we'll find an answer."*

*The second crow tried to push the pitcher over, straining with all of his might. But it was too heavy to budge. "It's hopeless!" he croaked, and flew away to look for water elsewhere.*

*But the first crow stayed by the pitcher and thought, and after a time it had an idea. Picking up some small pebbles in its beak, it dropped them one by one into the pitcher until at last the water rose to the brim. Then the clever bird happily quenched its thirst.*

*Wisdom and patience succeed where force fails.*

*One of Aesop's Fables*

# Introduction

*Pothead, Stoner, Doper, Hippy, Cannabinoider –*

Four out of the five words listed above define a particular reality based on culture and language. The fifth word, the one you can't pronounce, is something new.

Almost all of us were born into "marijuana" prohibition, which began in 1937. That prohibition is coming to an end because of a new word you are going to be hearing with increasing frequency. The word is "cannabinoid." What a cannabinoid is and does is the focus of this book – but you should know that we started with the intention of writing a "cannabis" book. As some of you are aware, there are plenty of great marijuana and cannabis books. Liberty is a common theme to these books as well as the healing powers of the plant. What hasn't been noted or described in context is the fundamental role cannabinoids play in life. Yes, life. Like the four out of five words mentioned above, and the cultural baggage they carry, clarity is needed to address some old misconceptions, demonizations, and prejudices built around the policy of marijuana prohibition – which is simply a cannabinoid prohibition – which makes it a life prohibition.

There is another important change. We have a President who won an election based on the idea of change – even change we can believe in. The President of the United States is referred to by the acronym "POTUS" (www.potus.com). Based on the changing scientific evidence, we believe this POTUS is going to end cannabis prohibition – that's right, the end is near, and here is one of the main reasons why: – Cannabis arrests went from just under 400,000 to nearly 750,000 by the last year of POTUS 42, Bill Clinton. That totals nearly five million fellow citizens arrested for cannabis violations under POTUS 42.

During POTUS 43, George W. Bush's administration, annual cannabis arrests remained at the 750,000 level through 2006. In 2007 and 2008 arrests topped 800,000. That totals over six million citizens arrested for cannabis under POTUS 43.

Now to Barack Obama and POTUS 44 – Will the legacy of his administration be more arrests given that cannabinoids are proving to be one of nature's best-kept secrets? – Or will POTUS 44 end the madness of arresting millions of fellow citizens for possessing cannabinoid plant material? – The writings contained in this book are in support of ending this madness. But more than that, while researching and writing this book, we learned how natural and vital cannabinoids are to human life. This project started as a book about cannabis but morphed into a book about cannabinoids – the scientific and Internet search term for the chemicals in the cannabis plant and our bodies.

The first thing we learned together – our first truth – was that every human being uses cannabinoids. We don't mean everyone smokes pot. No. What we mean is that ***cannabinoids and the endocannabinoid system (ECS) modulate other systems within the human body***. This is true for all mammals. Cannabinoids are shown to protect and heal other systems – such as the muscular, nervous, immune, reproductive and digestive. Essentially, modulation means that cannabinoids help other systems in the body adjust to changing conditions.

In the first part of the book we discuss basic scientific findings and the dynamic nature of cannabinoids. You will read how cannabinoids complete the human experience and begin to see what we are up against – the cognitive dissonance of describing 'marijuana' as something good. But slang terms like marijuana, pot, Mary Jane, reefer, etc., are cultural identifiers and not scientific. As cultural terms, we are not against the words marijuana and pot – we've only learned that there is greater clarity in the words cannabis and cannabinoids. That is because they are the words of science and <u>not</u> slang. We know you will have questions – like we did – and this book will provide the answers or point you in the direction the scientific evidence leads. And we are sure you will be surprised – *be you pothead or prohibitionist* – as you'll discover irrefutable truths that have been known for some time but hidden by the language games of our culture.

But think of it – after more than 70 years, wouldn't now be a good time for change and the truth about cannabis and cannabinoids? The truth of how cannabinoids help chemotherapy patients recover. The truth of how cannabinoids modulate the runner's high and physical activity. The truth of how cannabinoids protect the beginning of human life – the fertilized egg in the mother's womb. Or even the truth of taxing and regulating a cannabis economy instead of arresting millions of fellow citizens every presidential administration – which exposes another truth – the forgotten devastation of families affected by a cannabis arrest.

Any student of history can tell you we are not the first Americans to confront untruths. To voice our truth through language, to create a new set and setting, we turned to a collection of essays known as *The Federalist Papers*. During 1787 and 1788, James Madison, John Jay, and Alexander Hamilton wrote 85 essays in support of the US Constitution. They used the penname "Publius" in honor of a famed Roman republican – someone they saw as a defender of liberty. We are "Publius" in 2009-11 for the same purpose – to make our sum greater than our individual parts.


### *Life, Liberty and the Pursuit of Happiness*

Science is the language of Publius. It is science that can lift the fog of war caused by 70 years of Reefer Madness. As the founders detailed the workings of the US Constitution, piece-by-piece and Article-by-Article, we have given the same care and effort to describing the cannabis plant and the role of cannabinoids in our culture. We also found that cannabinoids shared one other strong characteristic from the founding period; the similarity is found in the famous phrase summing up the basic rights of free people – *Life, Liberty and the Pursuit of Happiness.*

It is no secret that many people think that there is a life-giving quality to cannabis use. That is where we began – the anecdotal and lived cannabinoid experience. Since the 1970s, cannabis use has been defined by practice – some combination of the medical/patient model and the recreational/liberty model. ***What we are describing is something new – the idea that cannabinoids are fundamental to life.*** The cannabis war will no longer be about use and ideology – about who is sick enough or free enough or responsible enough. What is new today is the science of cannabinoids – and you'll find it more than compelling – some even mind-blowing.

Liberty provides its own compelling arguments. The war on cannabis users has compromised our liberty. It has been this way so long that many of us don't even recognize the unintended consequences placed on our collective liberty by cannabis prohibition – the collateral damage caused by the war. But as this changes, as cannabis prohibition comes to a close, we can look forward to a better culture – one with fewer invasions of privacy, fewer arrests, fewer imprisonments – and more choices for relaxation, more affordable wellness and healthcare, more tax revenues, and, dare we say it – happier citizens. The days of Reefer Madness, when it was believed that marijuana smoking created homicidal maniacs, are behind us. The days of dominant Cheech and Chong images and spaced-out tokesters are behind us. Clearer perceptions about cannabis are emerging. Someone like Montel Williams is the new face of the cannabis patient – a former Marine and successful talk show host who fights Multiple Sclerosis and maintains his health and happiness through the use of cannabinoids. Or even beyond any medical perception, someone like Rick Steves – a successful writer and host of travel shows on television and radio. Or even beyond celebrity – perhaps someone like you?

That brings us to happiness. – Each individual citizen has their own definition of what makes them happy. Notice that the goal is not the "right to be happy" but the *pursuit* of happiness. This pursuit is intrinsically related to freedom of choice – the right to pursue one's happiness without infringing upon another's right to Life, Liberty and the Pursuit of Happiness. One doesn't have to be a lawyer to understand this is a legal problem – but it is also more than a legal problem. What we have, and what most of us have been born into, is a system that makes the pursuit of happiness a legal problem – one to be policed. This is a relatively new phenomenon. *Americans have not always thought the pursuit of happiness was something best handled by the courts.* At one time we believed in the **"right to be let alone."** In 1928, nine years before cannabis prohibition began, US Supreme Court Justice Louis Brandeis wrote of our constitutional right to be let alone in the case of *Olmstead v. U.S.*:

> The makers of our Constitution undertook to secure conditions favorable to **the pursuit of happiness.** They recognized the significance of man's spiritual nature, of his feelings and his intellect. They knew that only a part of the pain, pleasure and satisfaction of life are to be found in material things. They sought to protect Americans in their beliefs, their thoughts, their emotions and their sensations. They conferred, as against the Government, *the right to be let alone* – the most comprehensive of rights and the right most valued by civilized men.

The war on cannabis has been an assault on the right to be let alone. This means it is also an attack on the conditions favorable to the pursuit of happiness. Cannabis prohibition has contributed to a net loss of life, liberty and the pursuit of happiness. That is about to change. The end of cannabis prohibition is upon us because of its own logic – it should have worked by now.

One more thing: like life, liberty and the pursuit of happiness, I, Publius, have many forms – many selves, if you will. In reading *The Cannabis Papers*, you will find that I speak in many voices. That is because there are many voices to be heard. So take this book as the founders might have – and you'll see that the fog of war is not coming from the cannabis plant.

*Publius*

*Publius 2009-11* is Bryan Brickner, Julie Falco, Stephen Young, William Abens, Danielle Schumacher, Derek Rea (1954-2008), David Nott, Dan Linn, Dan S. Wang, Brian Allemana, Dianna Lynn Meyer, and many others.

# Part One:  Life


*In all we do, we must remember that the best healthcare decisions are not made by government and insurance companies, but by patients and their doctors.*

POTUS 43, George W. Bush
2007 State of the Union Address

#1

# Nature's (legal) cannabinoids

*"Where do you get 'it' from?"*

Most patients don't get asked where they get their medicine. That's because everyone knows people get their medicine from a pharmacy. But I have to get my medicine otherwise. I have to safeguard my "source" because my medicine is cannabinoid based – and that makes it almost illegal. – But not today. Today I can answer the source question openly because it is my local pharmacy – with drive-thru service and open to dispense medicine 24-hours a day. I drive up and push a big, yellow smiley-faced button to gain access – a soft automated voice comes over the speaker to verify that I am in the right place in order to pick up my prescription. Next, the typical professional looking person (white-coat with badge) slides open the window asking my name and what I need.

"I'm picking up a prescription for Publius."

They return with a baggie and bottle containing 30 synthetic cannabinoid capsules dosed at 5mg each – that's right, legal cannabinoids!

What are cannabinoids? Well, here is where things get interesting. As one learns in biology, the human body has many systems – the circulatory, respiratory, digestive, and nervous systems to name a few. Each system has parts; for example, the nervous system is made up of the brain, spinal cord and nerves. By the late 1980s, science identified a new human system – *the endocannabinoid system (ECS) – also referred to as the cannabinoid system.* There is a cannabinoid system present in all mammals – to include humans and 15,000 other species. A mammal is any vertebrate animal distinguished by self-regulating body temperature, hair, and milk-producing females – as mammal means "breast" or of the breast.

The ECS has two main parts: cannabinoids, which are chemical neurotransmitters, and two receptors called "CB1" and "CB2." Cannabinoids activate receptors found throughout the body – in all organs, for example. In fact, all systems in our bodies are *modulated* by the cannabinoid system. This means that as a body system changes, it uses the ECS to do so.

Science and popular search sites like Wikipedia use three classifications of cannabinoids:

1. *Endogenous cannabinoids* (also referred to as endocannabinoids), which are produced by the human body
2. *Herbal cannabinoids*, the kind found in the *cannabis sativa* plant
3. *Synthetic cannabinoids*, produced and distributed by pharmaceutical companies

The third kind is what I am picking up from the pharmacy – 30 Marinol (Dronabinol) capsules. Marinol is a prescribed cannabinoid from my doctor – and I am going to test it against the herbal cannabinoids I have been baking into my brownies for five years now.

The pharmacist hands me a white paper bag containing the Marinol prescribed for my Multiple Sclerosis (MS). Stapled to the top is a typical handout with cautionary medical information. The small amount (150mg) of the synthetic cannabinoid THC costs $370 – or more than $69,000 per ounce!

I sign my name on a distribution sheet and pay my $3 Medicare co-pay. The government, meaning our tax dollars, pays the other

$367 for my medicine. Now I am ready to go – but not before my 'synthetic cannabinoid' dealer informs me of possible side effects. She warns me to be on the lookout for – "dizziness, drowsiness, confusion, feeling 'high,' an exaggerated sense of well-being, lightheadedness, headache, red eyes, dry mouth, nausea, vomiting, stomach pain, clumsiness, or unsteadiness."

Geez – sounds like a lot of potential adversity on my chemically sensitive body. From personal experience, I know that the herbal cannabinoids do not cause these side effects in my body. The pharmacist did mention one noticeable side effect that I have had with eating cannabis brownies: dry mouth – which is hardly a problem when considering the overall benefits of the medicine.

When I get home I open the bag to take a look at the Marinol. The pills are a deep maroon color and perfectly round. They remind me of Boston Baked Beans – as they look exactly like those candies. One thing is for sure; synthetic cannabinoids do not look anything like herbal cannabinoids. The distinct medical difference of popping pills versus the variations and qualities of consuming natural cannabis cannot be understated – and surely won't be by me. After a week of taking one pill a night before bed, as the doctor prescribed, I do not notice any positive effects from the Marinol. It makes me hungry – but that was never a problem in the first place. But it is my first legal cannabinoid and that is what counts, right? – Not whether it works, just whether it is legal, right?

Wrong.

Here is what I know. I have been self-medicating with herbal cannabinoids for five years to provide relief from MS, which I have had for 23 years. During that time I went through the long list of prescribed pharmaceuticals. The relief was minimal. The problem was (and is) the side effects, which became unbearable over time. I felt like a slave, dependent on a cycle of pharmaceutical use which abused my body and left me in the most depressed, hopeless and flattened state.

I finally said enough of the pharma-tinkering with my body and my MS and tried baking herbal cannabinoids into brownies. In doing so, my alternative treatment made me a criminal. I began to eat a small cube of cannabis brownie three times a day. Within the first month my insomnia disappeared, my bladder issues calmed, nerve tingles of the arms, legs, and feet stilled. I was no longer breaking out in upper body tremors after being out in the world of loud noises, traffic, and the everyday racing of life. The MS was quieter. I found I wasn't contemplating suicide and I felt hopeful about my life again – but realized I had become a chronic criminal.

Cannabinoids are clearly medicinal to our bodies. But there is a strange distinction between which cannabinoids are effective and which ones are legal. In the case of my MS, appetite stimulation has not been a problem – which is what the Marinol is usually prescribed for. Marinol simply did not work for me. There are other pharmaceutical cannabinoids – such as Nabilone and Sativex – available in other countries, but they remain expensive and less effective than herbal cannabinoids. Nature created cannabis and the mammalian ECS, not you or me – and it was through the use of herbal cannabinoids that I was able to wean myself from a life of pharma-cocktails and move toward a healthier life. – Just as nature designed.

*Publius*
*(2009)*

### Search terms
Endocannabinoid system; endogenous, herbal, and synthetic cannabinoids; Marinol; Nabilone; Sativex; Multiple Sclerosis and cannabinoids.

### Research and selected readings
1998-present: International Association for Cannabinoid Medicines (IACM).

2003-2006: *O'Shaughnessey's* – Journal of the California Cannabis Research Medical Group.

2004: V Di Marzo, *Cannabinoids,* Kluwer Academic/Plenum Publishers, New York NY.

2002: M Earleywine, *Understanding marijuana: a new look at the scientific evidence*, Oxford University Press, New York NY.

2001 (1998): C Ratsch, *Marijuana medicine: a world tour of the healing and visionary powers of cannabis*, Healing Arts Press, Rochester VT.

1998: B Potter and D Joy, *The healing magic of cannabis*, Ronin Publishing, Berkeley CA.

1977 (1971): L Grinspoon, *Marihuana Reconsidered*, Harvard University Press, Cambridge MA.

#2

# Should pregnant women ~~smoke~~ consume pot?

*Uterine cannabinoids and the beginning of human life*

"Do you want pregnant women to smoke pot?"

That question bounced around the room (and in my head) for a moment. And the answer is an equivocal "Yes" – but the reason why I hesitate is the word "smoke."

Here's a better question – "Do you want pregnant women to consume cannabinoids?" The answer to that question might surprise you, but this is too important of an issue to be wrong – no matter what misconceptions one might have. But current research is confirming a new theory: **cannabinoids play a fundamental role in a healthy and successful pregnancy**.

First of all, there is no such thing as a drug-free pregnancy. The making of a baby is a biological and chemical phenomenon that every adult is somewhat familiar with. We know cells divide, organs grow, parts mature, and then birth – and the mystery of fertility goes on.

But one aspect of fertility is becoming significantly less mysterious. A 2006 report from the Pediatrics Department at Vanderbilt University characterized endocannabinoids as "an emerging concept in female reproduction." Why such praise? Because of what they found: a "cannabinoid sensor" mechanism to influence crucial steps during early pregnancy.

Pregnancy is a stress to the body. To modulate that stress, the ECS responds by creating endocannabinoids – the body's version of "first responders." By first responders I am referring to what the Vanderbilt research termed the "endocannabinoid signaling in preimplantation embryo development and activation." One of the first things the fertilized embryo must do is to attach itself to the lining of the uterus. Without becoming attached to the uterine wall, which forms the umbilical cord, there will be no pregnancy. Here is where cannabinoids play a key role: for the embryo to become attached to the lining of the uterus, a particular range (or amount) of one specific endocannabinoid, called *anandamide*, is necessary. This cannabinoid uses the CB1 receptors that are on the blastocyst (fertilized egg) – the same type of receptors that the herbal cannabinoid THC uses. The Vanderbilt research shows that if there is not enough anandamide (or too much), the embryo will not become attached to the uterine lining. Here is the visual representation presented by the Vanderbilt research team:[1]

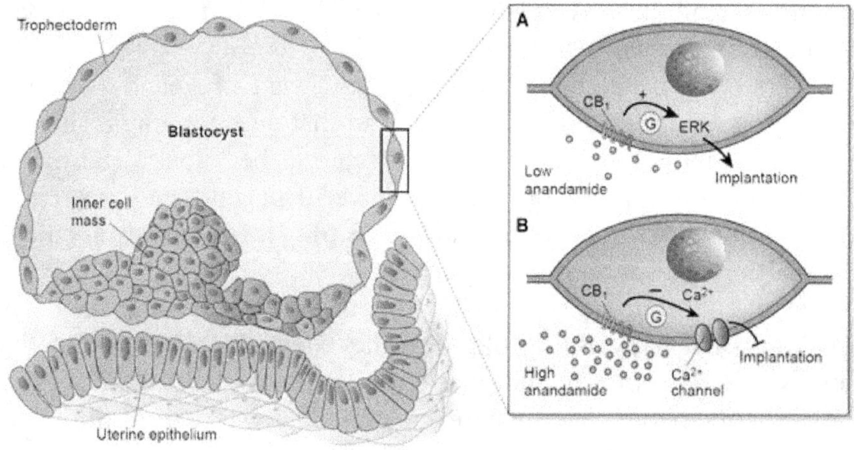


The Vanderbilt research shows how the fertilized egg is dependent on a functioning ECS – and specifically, the

---

[1] Endocannabinoid signaling directs peri-implantation events, *AAPS J, Wang H., Xie H., and Dey SK., Pediatrics Vanderbilt University, 2006.*
http://www.aapsj.org

endocannabinoid anandamide and the CB1 receptor. To make this more charming and less scientific, one could say that *once upon a time* there was a baby Publius. And before I was a baby, before even a fetus or an anything – there was this one sperm that was part of making me – and it was the smallest cell in the human body, only swimming 3mm a minute. And that single cell had a ways to travel. The journey to conception begins in one organ and ends up in another – from gonads to vagina, passing through the cervix, the uterus, and into a fallopian tube where the smallest human cell joins with the largest – my mother's egg. So the sperm and the egg meet and the rest is . . .

No – that is not the rest of the story. Until the now fertilized egg attaches itself to something, in this case, the lining of the uterus, there is no viable pregnancy – just a fertilized egg. That is why the Vanderbilt research is important. It points to a revolution in our way of thinking about cannabis and the cannabinoids it contains. For example, a fertilized egg is cannabinoid dependent. It, the life of the egg and the beginning of a viable pregnancy, depends on a healthy ECS. It takes the right amount of cannabinoids to activate a certain number of CB1 receptors in order for the fertilized egg to attach itself to the uterus. This process is accomplished because there are CB1 receptors on the *blastocyst* – that is, on the fertilized egg itself – and the cannabinoid anandamide on the endometrium – the inner lining of the uterus.

Cannabinoids not only play a role in the first responses of the body to fertility, but they also play a role in other aspects of pregnancy as well. A 2004 study published in the *American Journal of Obstetrics and Gynecology* concluded: "Both endogenous and exogenous cannabinoids exert a potent and direct relaxant effect on human pregnant myometrium, which is mediated through the CB1 receptor." This means that the middle layer of the uterine wall, the "myometrium," is modulated by cannabinoids as well. – And as a reminder, these uterine CB1 receptors are activated by endocannabinoids as well as herbal and synthetic cannabinoids.

In addition to conception, another 2004 report showed that endocannabinoids activate the oral motor musculature necessary for newborn mice to nurse – which makes sense because breast milk contains endocannabinoids. The same 2004 study also stated "Anandamide has neuroprotectant properties in the developing postnatal brain." And of course, all of this is new, right? – No. Fourteen years ago, in 1995, there was lab research on mice that showed that the mammalian ECS is involved in signaling within the uterus.

So let's review: cannabinoid receptors are located on the blastocyst, the fertilized egg, making the implantation of the egg cannabinoid dependent. We've also learned that throughout pregnancy and during nursing that the ECS delivers relief and neuroprotection to mother, fetus, and baby. That sounds pretty important – important enough to rethink the guilt, fear, shame, hesitation, and reticence of using cannabis to modulate the ECS before, during, and after pregnancy – as it seems that nature thought of it way before we did.

And no, pregnant women don't have to smoke blunts or joints to get their cannabinoids. Simply put, expectant mothers and new moms could consume cannabinoids in baked goods or whatever form is best for them. ***Harm reduction is the key.*** Perhaps in the future the health of a woman's ECS, and its effects on fetus and baby, will be the focus of pregnancy and not the fear mongering of "smoked marijuana." In the future, mothers-to-be might want to start asking their doctors something like, "How are my anandamide levels? – Too high or too low?" Or perhaps even more likely, maybe the doctors will be asking the mothers, "Have you had your cannabis brownie today?"

*Publius*
(2009)


**Search terms**
Uterine cannabinoids; anandamide; CB1 receptors; neuroprotection cannabinoids; breast milk (prolactin, oxytocin and cannabinoids); Kristen Peskuski; Ester Fride (1953-2010).

**Research and selected readings**

2009: A Langer-Gould, et al, *Exclusive breastfeeding and the risk of postpartum relapses in women with multiple sclerosis*, Archives of Neurology, August 2009:66(8):958-63.

2008: E Fride, *Multiple roles for the endocannabinoid system during the earliest stages of life: pre- and post-natal development*, Endocrinology, May 2008:20 Suppl 1:75-81.

2007: P Berghuis, et al, *Hardwiring the brain: endocannabinoids shape neuronal connectivity*, May 2007:316(5828):1212-6.

2007: T Harkany, et al, *The emerging functions of endocannabinoid signaling during CNS development*, Trends in Pharmacological Sciences, February 2007:28(2):83-92.

2006: H Wang, et al, *Endocannabinoid signaling directs peri-implantation events*, American Association Pharmaceutical Scientists, 2006:8(2):425-32.

2004: E Fride, *The endocannabinoid-CB(1) receptor system in pre- and postnatal life*, European Journal of Pharmacology, October 2004:500(1-3):289-97.

2004: M Dennedy, et al, *Cannabinoids and the human uterus during pregnancy*, American Journal of Obstetrics and Gynecology, January 2004:190(1):2-9.

2001: B Paria, et al, *Dysregulated cannabinoid signaling disrupts uterine receptivity for embryo implantation*, Biological Chemistry, June 2001:276(23):20523-8.

1995: S Das, et al, *Cannabinoid ligand-receptor signaling in the mouse uterus*, Proceedings of the National Academy of Sciences USA, May 1995:92(10):4332-6.

1994: M Dreher, et al, *Prenatal marijuana exposure and neonatal outcomes in Jamaica: an ethnographic study*, Pediatrics – American Academy of Pediatrics, February 1994:93(2):254-60.

#3

# Sporting cannabinoids

*Sweating ourselves high*

Wow. I just got back from a run and feel great. Not a difficult run – just wanted to break a sweat.

It seems that everyone advocates exercise. Few people argue against being active – but what is it that makes us feel so good? – And does us so much good? What chemicals in our body put a bounce in our step and a smile on our face? Try it – try bringing this up in a discussion and see how many people guess wrong. Ask them what chemical compound in the body accounts for the "runner's high"? – Those moments of time, both during and after physical activity, when one feels good and high.

People will typically guess endorphins as the answer. Say yes, endorphins are good, but have problems crossing the all-important "blood-brain barrier." So if endorphins can't get into the brain, they can't account for the high. But before the answer, let's have some fun and listen to POTUS 43, George W. Bush, and see how he describes the benefits of running. In an October 2002 interview for *Runner's World*, POTUS 43 was asked, "What role does running play in your mental and physical fitness?" He said it was very important and that he runs five or six times a week. President Bush went on to say that running:

- "helps me sleep at night"
- "keeps me disciplined"
- "breaks up my day"
- "allows me to recharge my batteries"
- "enables me to set goals – "
- "– and push myself toward those goals"
- "in essence, it keeps me young"
- "adds a little bounce to my step"
- "I get a certain amount of self-esteem from it – "
- "I just look and feel better"

Later in the interview President Bush is asked about running and how it helped him to quit drinking alcohol. POTUS 43 responded:

> "Definitely. As a runner, I quickly realized what it felt like to be healthy and I already knew what it felt like to be unhealthy. If you're drinking too much and you're running to cure a hangover, pretty soon you have to make a choice. ***Do you want to keep getting a hangover or do you want to feel the way you do after a run? So running is a way to heal people.*** Running is something that just makes you feel fantastic."

Yes, the ECS is a wonderful thing, and thank you for saying so President Bush – just like the 2003 research from the *NeuroReport: Cognitive Neuroscience and Neuropsychology*. This research from Georgia Tech and the University of California, Irvine, showed that a ***"class of chemicals known as cannabinoids may be the missing piece of the 'runner's high' puzzle long sought by scientists."***

That's right – the new runner's high theory is that the internal chemical system responsible is – the ECS.

Surprised? Well, you shouldn't be. Cannabinoids modulate the other systems in one's body. For example, breaking a sweat is an obvious bodily marker of this transition. In the moments when the body begins to adjust to the stress of running, the ECS is activated.

In the 2003 research, 24 male participants exercised for 45 minutes. They ran or cycled while the control group was at rest. All the runners and cyclists had "dramatically" elevated anandamide levels after 45 minutes of moderate exercise. From the *NeuroReport*: "Anandamide crosses the blood-brain barrier readily, avoiding the principal problem that plagued the endorphin hypothesis."

We will discuss the blatant irony of arresting over 800,000 fellow citizens for "exercising" their individual ECS by modulating their health with herbal cannabinoids – which is commonly referred to as "getting high." We'll discuss "high" as a concept later in the book, in the parts on Liberty and the Pursuit of Happiness. *For now, think of the foolishness of a sports dominated culture, one built on sweat and dependent on the ECS, and our herbal cannabinoid prohibition*. If humans did not have a cannabinoid system, we could not modulate the other systems. In playing a role in the modulation of other systems, the ECS helps our bodies adjust to changing circumstances – from heart-pumping running to chill-relaxing massage. Simply stated, cannabinoids work by adjusting the amplitude, frequency, and/or intensity of a nerve impulse.

– And POTUS 43 was a promoter of personal cannabinoid use, i.e., running, to the end. In 2007, Fred Barnes, executive editor of *The Weekly Standard*, wrote that President Bush stays healthy because of "his really good physical shape" and that exercise and sleep help to "keep his spirits **high**."

Yes, POTUS 43, we agree – and keep exercising! As POTUS 44 is also an advocate of exercise and physical activity – which has always been a pro-cannabinoid position!

*Publius*
(2009)


**Search terms**
Cannabinoids and exercise; runner's high; blood-brain barrier; Presidential physical fitness; POTUS 43 and alcohol.

**Research and selected readings**
2009: S Rossi, et al, *Exercise attenuates the clinical, synaptic and dendritic abnormalities of experimental autoimmune encephalomyelitis*, Neurobiology of Disease, October 2009:36(1):51-9.

2009: T Biro, et al, *The endocannabinoid system of the skin in health and disease: novel perspectives and therapeutic opportunities*, Trends in Pharmacological Sciences, August 2009:30(8):411-20.

2008: M Solinas, et al, *The endocannabinoid system in brain reward processes*, British Journal of Pharmacology, May 2008:154(2):369-83.

2008: L Chaitow, *Bodywork high: the cannabinoid connection*, Massage Today, February 2008:8(2).

2007: W Stern, *The General Motors: in Iraq with General Petreaus*, Runner's World, December 2007.

2004: A Dietrich and W McDaniel, *Endocannabinoids and exercise*, British Journal of Sports Medicine, 2004:38(5):536-41.

2004: A Burfoot, *Runner's High*, Runner's World, June 2004.

2003: P Sparling, et al, *Exercise activates the endocannabinoid system*, NeuroReport, December 2003:14(17):2209-11.

2002: Interview, *Running with President George Bush*, Runner's World, October 2002.

#4

# "DSI for Dummies"

*Getting to know cannabinoid history*

We've all seen those "_________ for Dummies" books. They're popular because they explain in detail complex subjects so that anyone can understand. That's what we're trying to do here, and with your ECS, we are going to help you overcome some of your federally imposed ignorance.

Of course, herbal cannabinoids have always been around. The scientific study of these substances began more than a hundred years ago. Beginning in 1896, some white-coats in Boston named Wood, Spivey, and Easterfield, isolated and named the first plant cannabinoid. Working with Indian hemp resin, also known as "charas," the authors described a "physiologically active substance" which they named Cannabinol (CBN).

About four decades go by with no advancement in the science, but many changes in the law. The Marihuana Tax Act of 1937 effectively began federal cannabis prohibition. – But the science continued. In 1939, one of America's leading organic chemists, Roger Adams, obtained a red oil extract made from Minnesota wild hemp supplied by the US Treasury Department. Adams, originally from Boston and a descendent of founder John Adams (VPOTUS 1 and POTUS 2), was working at the University of Illinois in

Champaign-Urbana. He is credited with the 1940 isolation and identification of the second plant cannabinoid – Cannabidiol (CBD).

It was twenty-four years until the next major discovery. In 1964, while working at Hebrew University in Jerusalem, Raphael Mechoulam identified the compound *delta-9-Snuffleupagus* – which became widely known as THC.

The identification of three plant cannabinoids is only half the initial history; finding the receptors completes this phase. Up until this point, it was thought that cannabis worked like alcohol. This all changed in 1988. Entering the brains of rats, scientists attached radioactive tags to synthetic cannabinoids and watched where they landed. They made an amazing discovery! They found two types of cannabinoid receptors in the body and named them "CB1" and "CB2." This discovery contrasts with alcohol, which has no receptors, is not part of a physiological system, and can easily induce alcohol poisoning.

Finding cannabinoid receptors in animals led scientists to an obvious question: what fits in them? This time they found the answer quickly. In 1992, the first endogenous cannabinoid was found by two scientists working in Mechoulam's Jerusalem laboratory. They discovered *"**anandamide**"* and named it after the Sanskrit word for **bliss**.

This history lesson brings us to the present topic – DSI. Let's break it down to its basics. DSI is an acronym for **<u>D</u>epolarized-induced <u>S</u>uppression of <u>I</u>nhibition**. This is one of the ways cells talk back to each other. This form of communication is the chemical process called "retrograde signaling." Imagine, like humans in conversation, cells have to let other cells know how things are going. Retrograde signaling filters and harmonizes this communication. It is when the receiving cell "talks back" and confirms to the sending cell that a message was received; the receiving cell also gives feedback on the original message. Think of this moment as a nod of understanding in a conversation, only at a cellular level.

In 2004, a *Scientific American* article titled "The Brain's Own Marijuana," put it this way – **"endogenous cannabinoids**

**participate in retrograde signaling, a previously unknown form of communication in the brain."** The phrase "previously unknown" explains a lot. That is why most Americans don't know anything about DSI, retrograde signaling, or the ECS. We've all been unaware and uninformed to a degree; – not to mention the lack of any major media coverage in the United States in response to these breakthrough discoveries.

We've already covered some amazing topics in this book. First, we discussed the three types of cannabinoids: endogenous, herbal and synthetic. We explained the importance of the ECS in successful fertility and pregnancy. We talked about how cannabinoids play a key role in the modulation of temperature and heart rate when jogging.

The beginning of this essay was a fill in the "___________" moment about DSI. This previously unknown signaling system appears to be fundamental to the evolution of species.

Now, about that *DSI for Dummies* book …

*Publius*
*(2009)*


### Search terms
DSI, retrograde signaling and cannabinoids; charas and cannabinol; Roger Adams and cannabidiol; Raphael Mechoulam, THC and anandamide; Sesame Streets' Snuffleupagus; DSE and cannabinoids; POTUS 2 John Adams.

### Research and selected readings
2010: P Zhu and D Lovinger, *Developmental alteration of endocannabinoid retrograde signaling in the hippocampus,* Neurophysiology, 2010:103:1123-9.

2006: Y Kawamura, et al, *CB1 receptor is the major cannabinoid receptor at excitatory sites in the hippocampus and cerebellum,* Neuroscience, March 2006:26(11):2991-3001.

2004: R Nicoli and B Alger, *The brain's own marijuana*, Scientific American, 22 November 2004.

2002: A Kreitzer and W Regehr, *Retrograde signaling by endocannabinoids*, Current Opinion in Neurobiology, 2002:12(3):324-30.

1992: W Devane, et al, *Isolation and structure of a brain constituent that binds to the cannabinoid receptor*, Science, December 1992:258(5090):1946-9.

1992: W Devane, et al, *A novel probe for the cannabinoid receptor [HU211]*, Medicinal Chemistry, May 1992:35(11):2065-9.

1988: W Devane, et al, *Determination and characterization of a cannabinoid receptor in rat brain*, Molecular Pharmacology, November 1988:34(5):605-13.

1964: R Mechoulam, et al, *Isolation, structure and partial synthesis of an active constituent of hashish*, American Chemical Society, 1964:86(8):1646-7.

1940: R Adams, et al, *Structure of cannabidiol (VI.), isomerization of cannabidiol to tetrahydrocannabinol, a physiologically active product,* American Chemical Society, September 1940:62(9):2402-5.

– R Adams, et al, *Structure of cannabidiol (I.), a product isolated from the marijuana extract of Minnesota wild hemp*, American Chemical Society, January 1940:62(1):196-200.

1896: T Wood, et al, *Charas: the resin of the Indian hemp*, Chemical Society, 1896:69:539-46.

#5

# Astrocytes and cannabinoids

*Reaching for the stars*

Science is filled with rat stories. Okay, more accurately, rodent tales. That's because rodents work so well in the lab replicating the research model. Scientists can take the same kind of rodent, rerun the same experiment, and be able to get the same results. They also often find major differences between species.

The CNS is a tightly regulated area of the body by design. Its functions are so crucial to life that a strong barrier exists to keep trespassers out. Cannabinoids are one of the few substances allowed into this exclusive VIP area. Nature created the ECS as a support system to intervene in signaling problems – such as *demyelination* and *apoptosis,* or "cellucide."

The familiar parts of the CNS are the brain and spinal cord. Only ten percent of the cells in the CNS are neurons – the other ninety percent are "glial," the Greek word for "glue." The most abundant glial cells in the CNS are star-shaped "**astrocytes**." These special glial cells help us keep it all together. They provide nutrients to nerves, are involved in cell impulse signaling, repair and induce scarring after inflammatory conditions, and support cells which form the blood-brain barrier.

A 2006 study found that human astrocytes are more advanced than rodents. Rat astrocytes protect and monitor approximately

100,000 synapses. Human astrocytes embrace "up to 2,000,000" synapses. This 20-times greater complexity led the researchers to identify human astrocytes as one of the "distinguishing cells" that separates us from rats.

Astrocytes play an essential role in the bodily process called "myelination." Our nerve axons are covered with myelin, an electrically insulating material which protects them. Myelin formation starts during fetal development and continues through adulthood. Research has established a working relationship between synaptic activity, astrocytes and myelination. Science also shows that the ECS supports astrocytes in building and repairing myelin. For example, astrocytes must produce proteins to initiate scarring as inflammation begins. Research from as long ago as 1998 found that cannabinoids potentiate astrocytes to produce the proteins needed to remedy the inflammation.

A 2008 study looked at how astrocytes and the ECS work together in another way. They found that hippocampal astrocytes have CB1 receptors on them that activate, stimulate and increase cellular processes. The research showed the existence of an "endocannabinoid-glutamate signaling pathway." In this pathway, astrocytes are a bridge for chemical (nonsynaptic) neuronal communication. Recall that each star cell is performing these tasks while simultaneously communicating with about two million other cells.

In 2010, the rat race research continued – this time with mice and the CB2 receptor. Activation of mice CB2 receptors was shown to prevent thermal pain, alleviate "allodynia," meaning abnormal pain, and facilitate the proliferation of anti-inflammatory glial signaling. Scientists used a synthetic cannabinoid called "NESS400" to investigate chronic pain thresholds. They looked at the CB2 and found that repeated treatment with NESS400 "significantly alleviated" nerve pain.

While astrocytes are repairing damaged nerve tissue, they are protected by the ECS. If astrocytes are not protected they will be unable to repair myelin. They also can't help with apoptosis, or cellucide. While most cells die a natural death, apoptosis is initiated, regulated and executed by the cell itself. In this case, astrocytes instruct cells <u>not</u> to kill themselves.

Surprise! Sometimes apoptosis is good – like if you're fighting cancer. The goal of chemotherapy is cancer cell death. Researchers are coming to the conclusion that cancer cannot be cured without the aid of the ECS. A simple search of the National Institutes of Health website (PubMed.gov) yields a vast array of studies validating the ECS's anticancer power. An example from 2010 – research published in the journal of Cancer Investigation shows that THC "inhibited [cancer] cell proliferation, migration and invasion, and induced cell apoptosis." ***That means THC killed cancer.*** – Which isn't a surprise: science discovered the same thing in 1975. See the article, "*Antineoplastic [anticancer] activity of cannabinoids*," from the National Cancer Institute, if you want to read it for yourself.

*Publius*
*(2010)*

### Search terms
Astrocytes, glial and cannabinoids; apoptosis and cannabinoids; myelin and cannabinoids; endocannabinoids and cannabinoids on PubMed.

### Research and selected readings
2011: A Verkhratsky, et al, *Where the thoughts dwell: the physiology of neuronal-glial "diffuse neural net,"* Brain Research Review, January 2011:66(1-2):133-51.

2010: M Navarrete and A Araque, *Endocannabinoids potentiate synaptic transmission through stimulation of astrocytes*, Neuron, October 2010:68(1):113-26.

2010: S Leelawat, et al, *The dual effects of delta(9)-tetrahydrocannabinol on cholangiocarcinoma cells: anti-invasion activity at low concentration and apoptosis induction at high concentration*, Cancer Investigation, May 2010:28(4):357-63.

2010: L Luongo, *1-(2',4'-dichlorophenyl)-6-methyl-N-cyclohexylamine-1, 4-dihydroindeno [1,2-c]pyrazole-3-carboxamide [NESS400], a novel CB2 agonist, alleviates neuropathic pain through functional microglial changes in mice*, Neurobiology of Disease, January 2010:37(1):177-85.

2009: A Verkhratsky, *Filming the glial dreams: real-time imaging of cannabinoid receptor trafficking in astrocytes*, American Society for Neurochemistry, 2009:1(5).

2008: M Navarrete and A Araque, *Endocannabinoids mediate neuron-astrocyte communication*, Neuron, March 2008:57(6):883-90.

2006: N Oberheim, et al, *Astrocytic complexity distinguishes the human brain*, Trends in Neuroscience, October 2006:29(10):547-53.

2006: T Ishibashi, et al, *Astrocytes promote myelination in response to electrical impulses*, Neuron, March 2006:49(6):823-32.

2002: L Walter, et al, *Astrocytes in culture produce anandamide and other acylethanolamides*, Biological Chemistry, June 2002:277:20869-76.

1998: F Molina-Holdago, et al, *The endogenous cannabinoid anandamide potentiates interlukin-6 production by astrocytes infected with Theiler's murine encephalomyelitis virus by a receptor-mediated pathway*, FEBS Letters, August 1998:433(1-2):139-42.

1975: A Munson, et al, *Antineoplastic [anticancer] activity of cannabinoids*, Journal of the National Cancer Institute, September 1975:55(3):597-602.

A HELPING
HAND
TERMINALLY ILL
6/2@2007
THE BUFFALO NEWS
WWW.ADAMZYGUS.COM
ADAM
ZYGUS

#6

# A medical cannabis club called CHAMP

*Publius visits California* ☺

At the 2002 NORML conference in San Francisco I met a "Harm Reduction Specialist" who changed my life. He worked at a medical cannabis club called CHAMP – *Californians Helping Alleviate Medical Problems*. The guy I met was Michael Barbitta, a walking-talking encyclopedia of information about cannabis. When he asked me if I would be interested in a tour of CHAMP, I knew this would be a once in a lifetime chance – and I quickly took him up on it.

After a short trip on BART, San Francisco's public transit system, we suddenly emerged in front of a building with the words – ***CHAMP, Service, Hope and Compassion*** – stenciled on the wall.

As we walked through the wrought iron front door, Mike is into an amazing nonstop discourse about the requirements of membership to CHAMP: valid CA State ID Card or CA Driver's license, plus a valid Medical Cannabis User ID Card with the physician's statement having been presented to receive the cannabis card. – Remember, this is California, where cannabis is legal under Proposition 215, the Compassionate Use Act (1996) – so, being from Illinois, it felt like another world to me.

Mike was on a roll as we climbed the stairs – CHAMP is a member funded, member run, nonprofit community wellness center – It is dedicated to the physical and mental health of the medical cannabis user – CHAMP believes medical necessity dictates that patients have safe access to cannabis – And that their cannabis be free of mold, mildew and pesticides.

We reach the top landing, and like he has recited a thousand times before, Mike points out the bulletin board and starts to answer the most commonly asked question before you have to ask: "The medicine provided by CHAMP is for medical use only and NOT for re-sale." A few introductions to the staff and we walk to the end of the counter. I try not to stare and be too obvious, or maybe it was just me, but I felt the most peaceful feelings I've ever experienced. This was no regular doctor's office. Here were comfortable chairs and couches, coffee tables with bowls filled with pretzels and popcorn and fresh fruit. There were a dozen or so people of various colors, ages and backgrounds sitting around chatting and enjoying one another's company. A woman nearby was preparing her meds to be used in a vaporizer – it looked like one of those Jiffy Pop bags – only filled with cannabinoids.

Then I remembered that this was a medical club. It made me wonder what they were talking about. – Cancer? – Chemotherapy? – The death or well-being of a friend? With those thoughts on my mind a moment of sadness sets in – but up pops Mike again. "Want a drink?" he asks. I looked at the can of Ensure in his hand and politely turned it down. Mike tosses the can to a guy sitting on a couch and he begins teaching me again. He describes the different types of medicine offered and says that some people have never used cannabis before, so teaching patients about their options is part of what CHAMP does. With decades of misinformation about marijuana, it is vital that people teach other people about cannabinoids and their healing properties.

I ask about the rules for purchase: "One ounce per person per day: – some come and make their purchase and leave, some stay because of the safe surroundings. We've learned that patients meeting together teach each other. They talk about how to take their medicines and which strains of cannabis work well. And it's good to hang out and share stories – it helps in the healing."

"How long can they hang out?"

"That depends – usually about an hour per day."

I ask Mike – "What if someone is all alone, broke and bedridden with no one to help them?"

Mike raises his eyes and looks straight into mine – "Yeah, we help them. I'll get on my bike and deliver it to them if I have to – that's what we do." As he was talking I recalled the words painted out front – ***Service, Hope and Compassion.***

This is a different and appealing kind of healthcare – one that develops our ability as humans to offer comfort, care, connection and compassion. In place of insurance forms, sterile rooms with staff going through the motions and making you feel less than human, at CHAMP one can just be and connect with other patients – with others who are working on healing. It is not the specialized offices of a cardiologist, neurologist, urologist, psychologist or ophthalmologist. At traditional healthcare facilities you feel separated from other patients. But here I saw individuals coming together to share in the healing. No matter the health issue, from cancer to the common cold, the ECS plays a role in our body of health – the same way a healthy digestive system does.

I take one last look around, thank the staff for their hospitality and down the stairs we go. In moments we are back out on the street and the spell broken – another reality. Damn, all the questions I wanted to make sure to ask started coming back to me. How long was I there? I look at my watch and figure about an hour – rules are rules.

I fly home to Illinois and have a hard time describing my CHAMP visit to myself – let alone my friends. I cannot find enough words to describe the care and compassion. Yeah, people were sitting around consuming cannabis, but that's not what it was about.

I guess it doesn't really matter what I felt at the time – as CHAMP was forced to close its doors by our federal government only a month after I visited. Now, more than seven years later, perhaps what mattered was what I experienced – and it changed my life.

*Publius*
*(2009)*

**Search terms**
California Proposition 215 (1996); Oregon & Colorado; cannabinoids and anticancer; AG Holder and cannabis; Michael Barbitta; Ed Rosenthal; Derek Rea (1954-2008).

**Research and selected readings**


2010: L Richmond, *What if cannabis cured cancer?* Documentary film.

2010: D Whyte, et al, *Cannabinoids inhibit cellular respiration of human oral cancer cells*, Pharmacology, 2010:85(6):328-35.

2009: M Salazar, et al, *Cannabinoid action induces autophagy-mediated cell death through stimulation of ER stress in human glioma cells,* Clinical Investigation, 2009:119(5):1359-72.

2008: P Massi, et al, *Expression and function of the endocannabinoid system in glial cells*, Current Pharmaceutical Design, 2008:14(23):2289-98.

2006: A Ligresti, et al, *Antitumor activity of plant cannabinoids with emphasis on the effect of cannabidiol on human breast carcinoma*, Pharmacology and Experimental Therapeutics, September 2006:318(3):1375-87.

2004: C Blazquez, et al, *Cannabinoids inhibit the vascular endothelial growth factor pathway in gliomas (brain tumors)*, Cancer Research, August 2004:64(16):5617-23.

1998: V Di Marzo, et al, *The endogenous cannabinoid anandamide inhibits human breast cancer cell proliferation*, Proceedings of the National Academy of Sciences USA, July 1998:95(14):8375-80.

1995: L Grinspoon, et al, *Marijuana, the AIDS wasting syndrome, and the US government*, New England Journal of Medicine, September 1995:333(10):670-1.

#7

# Chemotherapy and cannabinoids

*Fighting cancer is a fight for your life*

In 2005 at the age of 65, I was diagnosed with colon cancer and subsequently with lymph and liver cancer. That is a year I won't soon forget. When I realized the uphill battles I faced, I quickly determined I wanted to be a survivor, and my entire focus was on beating the cancers. My initial colon resection removed 23 cancerous lymph nodes and lesions. I then began a six-month regimen of chemotherapy prior to removal of half my liver in December – and back to chemo for an additional three months to ensure eradication.

Shortly before starting chemotherapy, I had a catheter implanted in my left arm. This made the hundreds of injections a lot less painful. The medical professionals were at their best, though my experience as a patient was chillingly lonely. My chemo routine was methodical. I went into the therapy center on alternate Wednesdays. I got a blood test. I filled out a form about what I was experiencing emotionally and physically. I sat in a chair for six hours while being injected with incredibly expensive chemo drugs. I also had to wear a pressurized bottle that injected a different chemo drug for two more days. I returned on Fridays to get unhooked from the bottle.

Wednesdays through Saturdays were usually better. On Sundays the nausea and diarrhea started and continued for about seven days. During this time I spent much of my day in bed – the term "sick as a dog" comes to mind. If you have ever experienced seasickness, imagine it combined with diarrhea and lasting for a week. (The "middle of the night while sleeping diarrhea" is downright embarrassing.) My doctor recommended anti-nausea medicine and I took up to 18 Imodium pills a day.

By Mondays and Tuesdays I generally felt stronger – then back to the center on Wednesday for more chemotherapy. Over the six months I had lost 40 pounds, some of my hair and basically looked and felt fatigued.

It was during this time that I was surprised when a close relative suggested that I try "marijuana" to relieve my symptoms. I did try it. Never having been a regular smoker of anything, the first few times I gagged from the smoke and vomited. I did notice my nausea had subsided and I attributed this fact to vomiting. As I became accustomed to taking smaller amounts of cannabis smoke more frequently, I learned to control my gag reflex. – That's when the amazement started: I would go from bed-ridden and nauseous to actually feeling fine in about ten minutes. – And yes, it felt like a miracle drug!

My enthusiasm was that of a born-again convert.

I wanted the world to know.

I wanted my fellow sufferers to know.

I wanted to share the discovery.

I wanted to tell everyone of an easy treatment that quickly relieved my symptoms.

I wanted to tell my doctor. I did. He obviously didn't want to hear about, nor comment on, my cannabis use. Crestfallen, I realized that he felt he could not. He too was a victim of the system – a victim of cannabis prohibition. My doctor wouldn't (or couldn't) discuss the healing effects of cannabinoids. We were at an impasse. The medicine that worked against the nausea was not discussable. The medicine that didn't control the nausea and made me feel worse, we were free to discuss. That was a perplexing moment: exactly when my life mattered most, I couldn't talk to my doctor about how I was staying alive.

Vital to chemotherapy is the ability to keep food down – to stay hydrated. Vomiting was the problem – cannabis was the solution. I wanted to talk to my doctor about my effective treatment. But couldn't.

Our government has historically denied patients and scientific evidence regarding the healing effects of cannabis and cannabinoids. The feds go so far as to say that no evidence exists that "marijuana" has any medical value, as evident in the retention of cannabis as a Schedule 1 narcotic. ***Given the scientific findings and research, this is willful ignorance.*** Anyone with a computer and Internet access can educate themselves about cannabinoids. Aren't federal officials capable of this?

Fourteen state governments have laws to protect patients, doctors and caregivers. In states such as Oregon, Colorado, and Michigan, dispensaries are opening and thousands of patients and caregivers are now protected by law. In the past, our government has harassed doctors, raided dispensaries and threatened patients in medical cannabis states. We are witnessing the transformation of this situation. As the founders envisioned, the citizens are leading – now it's up to the government to follow.

*Publius*
(2010)

### Search terms
Chemotherapy, cancers and cannabinoids; nausea; glioma; cannabidiol; vaporization; Americans for Safe Access (ASA).

### Research and selected readings
2010: M Niki, et al, *Reciprocal modulation of sweet taste by leptin and endocannabinoids*, Results and Problems in Cell Differentiation, 2010:52:101-14.

2010: R Yoshida, et al, *Endocannabinoids selectively enhance sweet taste*, Proceedings of the National Academy of Sciences USA, January 2010:107(2):935-9.

2009: N Olea-Herrero, et al, *Inhibition of tumor prostrate PC-3 cell growth by cannabinoids R (+) Methanandamide and JWH-015: involvement of CB2*, British Journal of Cancer, September 2009:101(6):940-50.

2008: K Gustafsson, et al, *Expression of cannabinoid receptors type 1 and type 2 in non-Hodgkin lymphoma: growth inhibition by receptor activation*, International Journal of Cancer, September 2008:123(5):1025-33.

2007: R Mechoulam, et al, *Cannabidiol – recent advances*, Chemistry & Biodiversity, August 2007:4(8):1678-92.

2007: G Velasco, et al, *Cannabinoids and gliomas*, Molecular Neurobiology, August 2007:36(1):60-7.

2005: D Zamora-Valdes, et al, *The endocannabinoid system in chronic liver disease*, Annals of Hepatology, Oct-Dec 2005:4(4):248-54.

2005: N Kogan, *Cannabinoids and cancer*, Mini Reviews in Medicinal Chemistry, October 2005:5(10):941-52.

2003: S Jones and J Howl, *Cannabinoid receptor systems: therapeutic targets for tumor intervention*, Expert Opinions on Therapeutic Targets, December 2003:7(6):749-68.

2001: V Di Marzo, et al, *Leptin-regulated endocannabinoids are involved in maintaining food intake*, Nature, April 2001:410(6830):822-5.

2000: D Piomelli, *Pot of gold for glioma therapy*, Nature Medicine, March 2000:6(3):255-6.

www.coxandforkum.com

#8

Patient patients

> *Why is patience considered the most powerful and difficult spiritual practice? – Because patience is the antidote to anger. When we're patient, we don't dance to the jerky, ever changing beat of worldly circumstances. Instead, we think, speak, and act in a measured way, as if to a steady, internal heartbeat – a tempo that comes from our deepest, most secret being. When we achieve this degree of patience, how can we get carried away by anger, much less rattled by petty irritations?*

> *"Buddha is as Buddha does" by Lama Surya Das*

Cannabis not only helps people with diseases and many different medical conditions – it is keeping some patients alive. I am 44 years old and have lived with MS for about half my life. During that time I've learned to be a patient *patient*. I took the advice of my doctors and the pharmaceuticals they prescribed. In an effort to manage my symptoms, I took one drug after another only to find the next nightmare of side effects crushing. This is why they call me a *patient* – I am supposed to endure, and if I am patient enough, there will be relief and a better quality of life.

I smoked what we called "marijuana" while in college, and stopped entirely as I entered the workforce. In 1998, after many failed pharmaceutical combinations, I smoked again for medicinal purposes. At that time, I noticed how it relieved my leg spasticity. MS causes the nerves to "misfire," making my legs twitchy and jumpy. The cannabinoids in cannabis eased this problem while also helping with my bouts of recurring insomnia.

It wasn't until I started eating cannabis brownies in 2004 that I noticed a number of additional benefits. I regained better control of my bladder and a "quieting" of the tingling and numbing pain – which is a constant symptom of MS.

I also found that activating the ECS with the cannabis brownies calmed me. For example, cannabinoids kept my nerves from overloading whenever I was in a crowded or loud place. Typically in these situations, my nerves would get too stimulated – which means my body would start to "crash," often resulting in tremors. It's similar to a computer crashing. By shutting the computer down it may restore the system; the way I restore is by finding a dark, quiet, calm space to "reboot" my system. These crashes were not just painful, they progressed the disease, as I could literally feel my nerves fraying.

Being an MS patient has taught me endurance. My ability to stand straight and tall or walk from place to place is dramatically improved with cannabis. My balance is more controlled and I can walk heel-to-toe. Without this medicine, I typically have to hold onto a walker while my locked-legs are dragged underneath as I lurch forward. With cannabis, on my best days, I can walk – heel-toe-heel-toe-heel-toe. My legs can relax when I stand. I'm able to start moving with a spry jaunt through my apartment. Compared to walking like the Tin Man wearing a suit of armor, I feel like I'm again in better control of my body.

Perhaps most importantly, since I started using cannabis brownies, my depression has ended. Depression itself makes MS worse by overstressing an already taxed immune system. The health of our immune system affects the central and peripheral nervous systems. Surrounding and protecting our nerve fibers, like a sheath of an electrical cord, is a fatty tissue called "myelin." Myelin helps nerve fibers conduct electrical impulses. In MS, myelin is lost in *multiple* areas, leaving scar tissue called *sclerosis*. When myelin is damaged, the ability of nerves to conduct electrical impulses is disrupted. This produces the various symptoms of MS. Recent science has shown that the endocannabinoid system actually helps myelin rebuild itself – a process called "remyelination." I guess that's why I'm less depressed.

In my journey I have learned a lot about patience. Although, the laws in most of the country make this medicine illegal and difficult to obtain, I am patiently waiting to be able to access cannabis as easily as the pharmaceuticals that failed to help the MS.

I want you to see my story as one of discovery and healing. Not all stories work out that way. Many patients before me have endured the consequences of cannabis prohibition: people have lost and are continuing to lose their lives. While we wait for the laws to change, patients have been dragged through the legal system and have been denied access to their medicine. One noted example is Jonathan Magbie – a 24-year old who died in 2004 while incarcerated in a Washington DC jail. He was serving a ten day sentence because he told a judge that he wouldn't stop using cannabinoids. Magbie was a quadriplegic patient and he smoked cannabis to ease the painful symptoms of his paralysis. At age four, while exiting a school bus, he was struck by a drunk driver. The accident left Magbie paralyzed from the neck down, stunting his growth and relegating him to a wheelchair for the rest of his life.

Magbie's healthcare should have been an obvious concern to the court. He was incapable of moving without the aid of a chin-operated wheelchair and required a tracheotomy tube, a pulmonary pacemaker, and a ventilator at night in order to breathe. Since he was not provided a ventilator in his jail cell, he contracted pneumonia. He had difficulty speaking above a whisper and was forced to bang his wheelchair around in order to get the attention of the corrections officers. Magbie's movement apparently irritated the guards, so they locked him inside an infirmary cell without access to a panic button. The guards did not check on Magbie until the next morning when they found him dead.

Dying alone in a jail cell is a long way from the day Magbie had his picture taken with POTUS 40, Ronald Reagan. We need much more than feel good pictures from our political leaders – we need new cannabis laws. I fear the day that I would be arrested and denied access to my medicine. No patient person should have to endure such injustice – in the name of justice.

*Publius*
(2010)

**Search terms**
CBs, myelin and remyelination; CBs and pain; Jonathan Magbie, Colbert King, and Reagan; 1998-Present DC Medical Cannabis; Dale Gieringer.

**Research and selected readings**
2011: *The Exile Nation Project: a film by Charles Shaw*, ExileNation.org.

2010: P Tyagi, et al, *Functional role of cannabinoid receptors in urinary bladder*, Indian Journal of Urology, Jan-Mar 2010:26(1):26-35.

2009: *Congress allows DC to implement 1998 medical marijuana law*, 9 December 2009: **Jonathan Magbie died in 2004.**

2009: P Anand, et al, *Targeting CB2 receptors and the endocannabinoid system for the treatment of pain*, Brain Research Review, April 2009:60(1):255-66.

2008: A Arevalo-Martin, et al, *CB2 cannabinoid receptors as an emerging target for demyelinating diseases: from neuroimmune interactions to cell replacement strategies*, British Journal of Pharmacology, January 2008:153(2):216-25.

2006: A Hohmann and R Suplita, *Endocannabinoid mechanisms of pain modulation,* American Association of Pharmaceutical Scientists, November 2006:8(4):E693-E708.

2005: C King, *A searing portrait of abuse*, Washington Post, 26 November 2005.

2003: A Arevalo-Martin, et al, *Therapeutic action of cannabinoids in a murine model of multiple sclerosis*, Neuroscience, April 2003:23(7):2511-6.

*Jonathan Magbie and POTUS 40 in 1982*

#9

# To sleep, perchance to dream –

*Shakespeare*

Doctors and poets agree to the necessary role of sleep and dreams to our health. Common sense suggests that they are essential to the human experience. This is confirmed by research which shows that sleep reduces stress, improves alertness and memory, helps repair the body, and restores one's spirit.

Our 24-hour culture is a challenge to the natural rhythms of our sleep-wake cycle, making it difficult to slow down and rest. This creates many sleep disorders. Most conventional sleep aids, prescription and non-prescription, are fraught with problems. Some are simply ineffective while others create dependency. This is because they miss the mark. They are not cannabinoid-based and do not activate the body's own sleep aid – the ECS.

> ***"Oh sleep, o gentle sleep,***
> ***Nature's soft nurse,***
> ***How have I frighted thee,***
> ***That thou no more wilt weigh my eyelids down***
> ***And steep my senses in forgetfulness?"***

There's the rub. Nature already provided us with a sleep aid – endocannabinoids and retrograde signaling. Once this system is activated, sleep can begin. My personal experience with sleep problems isn't uncommon. The use of cannabis to activate "*Nature's soft nurse*" eased the transition between consciousness and sleep.

Many people use cannabis for better quality sleep. They also report that the sleep experience is effective. This contrasts with the pharmaceuticals and their reported side effects – things like dizziness, symptoms of the common cold, and morning drowsiness. Nor do cannabinoids lead to frightening experiences of extended sleep walking or even more dangerously, to sleep driving. The intense desire for a normal night's rest makes people willing to endure such extreme side effects.

> *"Weary with toil,*
> *I haste to my bed,*
> *The dear repose for limbs with travel tired,*
> *But then begins a journey in my head,*
> *To work my mind when body's work's expired."*

The research on sleep and cannabinoids is more promising. The Chemistry & Biodiversity Journal reported in 2007 that patients given cannabis extracts experienced more restful sleep, an increase in their daytime level of function, and an improved quality of life. This study of 2,000 patients using a cannabinoid medicine found "marked improvement in subjective sleep parameters."

Americans spend nearly $3 billion annually on sleep medications. Millions more are spent selling pharmaceuticals to us. Our government has noticed. The National Institutes of Health (NIH) is calling for more research into insomnia and its treatments. Many drugs taken for insomnia have not been tested for long-term use, even though patients tend to take them for years. Furthermore, according to a recent NIH report, some commonly used treatments for sleeplessness — including antidepressants and antihistamines — are not approved for insomnia.

***"The pangs of despised love,***
***The law's delay,***
***The insolence of office,***
***And the spurns that patient merit . . ."***

More severe sleep disorders than insomnia exist. Sleep apnea is a disorder that affects 12 million Americans. It is characterized by frequent interruptions in breathing of up to ten seconds or more during sleep. The condition is associated with numerous physiological disorders, including fatigue, high blood pressure, heart attack, stroke and death.

Several years ago, in 2002, the Journal of the American Academy of Sleep Medicine reported beneficial results for cannabinoids on sleep-related apnea. Researchers at the University of Illinois-Chicago reported "potent suppression" of sleep-related apnea in rats given cannabinoids. They found that the herbal cannabinoid delta-9-THC and the endocannabinoid oleamide each stabilized respiration during sleep.

A 2008 review made it clear: "The activation of the CB1 receptor leads to an induction of sleep."

***"When day's oppression is not eased by night,***
***But day by night and night by day oppressed,"***

Recent research continues to confirm the relationship between cannabinoids and sleep. Talk to cannabis consumers about the quality of their sleep and you'll often hear positive responses. Anecdotally, I can attest to that. But then all good sleep is anecdotal. Just think of a friend "oppressed" from a sleep disorder, and imagine the relief a cannabis cookie could do before bedtime.

*"To be or not to be –*
*That is the question:*
*Whether 'tis nobler in the mind to suffer*
*The slings and arrows of outrageous fortune,*
*Or to take arms against a sea of troubles*
*And, by opposing, end them."*

*Publius*
(2010)

### Search terms
Oleamide; sleep regulation and CB1 receptor; sleep apnea and CBs; Shakespeare and cannabis; sleep-wake cycle; Dale Boger; Eric Murillo-Rodriquez; Ethan Russo.

### Research and selected readings
2010: A Herrera-Solis, et al, *Acute and subchronic administration of anandamide or oleamide increases REM sleep in rats*, Pharmacology, Biochemistry, and Behavior, March 2010:95(1):106-12.

2009: G Mueller and W Driscoll, *Biosynthesis of oleamide*, Vitamins and Hormones, 2009:81:55-78.

2009: E Murillo-Rodriquez, et al, *Mechanisms of sleep-wake cycle modulation*, CNS & Neurological Disorders Drug Targets, August 2009:8(4):245-53.

2008: E Murillo-Rodriquez, *The role of the CB1 receptor in the regulation of sleep*, Progress in Neuropsychopharmacology & Biological Psychiatry, August 2008:32(6):1420-7.

2007: E Russo, et al, *Cannabis, pain, and sleep: lessons from therapeutic clinical trials of Sativex®, a cannabis-based medicine*, Chemistry & BioDiversity, 2007:4:1729-43.

2003: V Di Marzo, *Manipulation of the endocannabinoid system by a general anaesthetic*, British Journal of Pharmacology, July 2003:139(5):885-6.

2002: D Carley, et al, *Functional role for cannabinoids in respiratory stability during sleep*, Sleep, June 2002:25(4):399-400.

1998: E Thomas, et al, *Oleamide-induced modulation of 5-hydroxytryptamine [5-HT] receptor-mediated signaling*, Annals of the NY Academy of Sciences, December 1998:861:183-9.

1998: D Boger, et al, *Oleamide: an endogenous sleep-inducing lipid and prototypical member of a new class of biological signaling molecules*, Current Pharmaceutical Design, August 1998:4(4):303-14.

1998: D Boger, et al, *Structural requirements for 5-HT2A and 5-HT1A serotonin receptor potentiation by the biologically active lipid oleamide*, Proceedings of the National Academy of Sciences USA, April 1998:95(8):4102-7.

1997: T Bisogno, et al, *The sleep inducing factor oleamide is produced by mouse neuroblastoma cells*, Biochemical and Biophysical Research Communications, October 1997:239(2):473-9.

1996: J Huidobro-Toro and R Harris, *Brain lipids that induce sleep are novel modulators of 5-hydroxytryptamine receptors*, Proceedings of the National Academy of Sciences USA, July 1996:93(15):8078-82.

# #10

# "Cannabinoids" succeed where "marijuana" fails

*The word war*

Words, be they new or old, both limit and extend thought. If we look at the word "Marijuana," we will find a popular term of culture that is common both on the street and in mass media. However, like the words *pot, dope, ganja, and reefer, marijuana* is slang and has little value in a discussion about medicine, policy and human life. And it is often used by prohibitionists as a weapon of propaganda, where a single mention of the weed can incite reefer madness.

When discussing law and science, cannabis and cannabinoids are the standard and accepted terms. If the word "marijuana" were to be used in a scientific setting, the word *"marijuana-noid"* would have to be coined to discuss the "marijuana-modulators" of the ECS.

Back in the day, Harry Anslinger and the prohibitionists (no it's not a band) put slang in the founding law of prohibition – the 1937 Marihuana Tax Act. Anslinger is the one person we can all thank for federal cannabis prohibition. He is known for wacky marijuana quotes. Many are racist in tone and emphasis. Here's one about the plant that makes marijuana-noids: *"Marijuana is an addictive drug which produces in its user's insanity, criminality and death."*

Anslinger's characterization of marijuana as understood in the 1930s crashes into our discussion of the ECS and cannabinoids. That's because the "evil of marijuana" is a cultural argument. Every scientific discussion in the 21$^{st}$ century uses the word "cannabinoid." Often, in legal and scientific fields, the word "marijuana" is used to conjure up reefer-madness-like fears and to distract from a serious policy debate. It would be like using the "N-word" – arguably our nation's most notorious slang word – to talk about legal and scientific policies regarding a group of Americans.

In the scientific community, there is clearly an opposite view. Tom Brock, a researcher for the pharmaceutical company Cayman Chemical, speaks highly of cannabinoids and what they do. In an essay titled *Cannabinoids: to the neurons and beyond,* he imagines the blessings of healthy cannabinoid receptors (cue Beatles' song):

> *Imagine what could be achieved if signaling through these receptors could be controlled: happy, slim, and healthy people who remember that they're pain-free.*

Well, as you can see, Brock has quite a different take than Anslinger did on these marijuana-noid thingies. Our **cannabinoider** asks us to imagine happy, slim and healthy people who remember they're pain-free. Our **prohibitionist** believes marijuana users are doomed addicted insane criminals. When reading Brock next to Anslinger, it's hard to imagine we are even discussing the same thing. In fact, we're not – the old saw marijuana as a deadly weed, the new as a promising plant. It's amazing what 70 years of experience and information will do.

There is also plenty of examples where the word "marijuana" is used in a joking way – just ask Cheech and Chong. Pharmaceutical, scientific and research communities don't think cannabinoids are a joke. Back in the early days of Mary's prohibition, no one knew humans had an ECS; now we even know how the body *produces* endocannabinoids. In 2009, Cayman Chemical published a 56-page cannabinoid marketing and research booklet. In it, Publius first learned of the two enzymes – *DAG lipase alpha and beta* – which the body needs to produce the endocannabinoid 2-AG, a cannabinoid fundamental to retrograde signaling. And this is no joke.

Translation according to Publius: $a + b$ = 2-AG. This means two enzymes naturally come together to modulate cell signaling. Think of it as a relay race where 2-AG is the **informational baton**. Brock's research company is investigating ways to increase this relaying of information. They are trying to extend-and-enhance the half-life and travel time of 2-AG. – Why?

Because scientists understand that *cannabinoids are good*. They are working from the premise that our ECS has therapeutic value. Brock and the white-coats believe these include: **"reduced anxiety, reduced sensitivity and dependence to alcohol and nicotine, less age-related cardiac dysfunction, increased memory acquisition and extinction, and protection against neurodegeneration."** One using the cultural term "marijuana" to understand and explain these biological processes will fail.

Defeating things like Alzheimer's is where cannabinoids are likely to succeed. Alzheimer's is a neurodegenerative disorder that steals and destroys one's ability to have a peaceful end to life. Little is understood about preventing or healing this disease. What is clear, according to the scientific data, is that the ECS is part of any solution. For example, a 2005 review found that *"cannabinoids succeed in preventing the neurodegenerative process occurring in [Alzheimer's] disease."* A 2008 review came to the same conclusion – highlighting the fact that cannabinoids *"represent an endogenous adaptive response aimed at counteracting"* the underlying causes of Alzheimer's.

The horizon looks bright as well. Beyond supporting our basic health, studies show that cannabinoids increase *neurogenesis* – the process by which we grow brain cells. Current research suggests the CB2 receptor *"may assist in the treatment of neuropathologies by increasing neurogenesis."*

The shift is here – from slang to science, from marijuana to cannabinoids. Marijuana will remain a cultural icon, but please keep politics out of the petri dish. This plant may save your life one day.

*Publius*
*(2010)*

**Search terms**
Alzheimer's disease and cannabinoids; Cayman Chemical and cannabinoids; neuroprotection and cannabinoids; neurogenesis, hippocampus and cannabinoids; CB2 receptor and neurogenesis; George Lakoff.

**Research and selected readings**
2010: J Rivers and J Ashton, *The development of cannabinoid CBII receptor agonists for the treatment of central neuropathies*, Central Nervous System Agents in Medicinal Chemistry, March 2010:10(1):47-64.

2009: T Brock, *Cannabinoids: to the neurons and beyond*, Neuroscience Vol. 3: Cayman Chemical.

2009: Y Marchalant, et al, *Cannabinoids attenuate the effects of aging upon neuroinflammation and neurogenesis*, Neurobiology of Disease, May 2009:34(2):300-7.

2009: B Basavarajappa, et al, *Endocannabinoid system: emerging role from neurodevelopment to neurodegeneration*, Mini Reviews in Medicinal Chemistry, April 2009:9(4):448-62.

2008: T Bisogno and V Di Marzo, *The role of the endocannabinoid system in Alzheimer's disease: facts and hypotheses*, Current Pharmaceutical Design, 2008:14(23):2299-3305.

2007: I Galve-Roperh, et al, *The endocannabinoid system and neurogenesis in health and disease,* Neuroscientist, April 2007:13(2):109-14.

2005: B Ramirez, et al, *Prevention of Alzheimer's disease pathology by cannabinoids: neuroprotection mediated by blockade of microglial activation*, Neuroscience, February 2005:25(8):1904-13.

# #11

## Washington's hemp seed love

I was in Polo, Illinois talking hemp with retired farmer Paul Fossler, who had the rare experience of legally growing hemp (cannabis). Fossler wasn't merely allowed to grow hemp – he was encouraged by the US government during World War II. His interview appears in a documentary on the subject called *Government Grown: How Polo Illinois Helped Win the War*. Like fellow farmer George Washington, Fossler grew hemp for the good of his country.

Why hemp? – **Because it's awesome**. It can be used for clothing, food and fuel without negative environmental effects. Those facts have been known for thousands of years. Today hemp seed is hailed as a **superfood** because of its ratio of Omega-3 to -6 fats – though it's illegal for American farmers to grow it. Making hemp legal for farming is obvious. That's not our seed of dispute; instead, we want to direct your attention to Washington's hemp farming, and in particular, *his hemp seed love*.

The seeds from the hemp plant have been a superfood in any century (not just our own). Washington harvested these seeds for 34 years. He first grew hemp in 1765 – more than a decade before becoming a revolutionary. At this time he was a Virginian, an elite plantation owner, and a subject of the King of England. As we talk about his hemp seed love, keep in mind Washington's slaves were working his hemp fields.

Hemp was grown in Virginia from its founding; in 1607 colonists were harvesting fiber and seed. A dozen years later it was mandated that every colonist grow 100 plants to support the colony – with the Governor boasting he would grow 5,000!

Washington became familiar with hemp in 1765 as he began to grow it as a cash crop. He was making some money growing tobacco and shipping it to London markets. But tobacco farming was depleting his soil – something hemp wouldn't do.

His need for another cash crop coincided with the British Empire's call for hemp. The King and Parliament passed a law putting a **"bounty" on hemp**. A bounty was an extra payment for a crop deemed beneficial to the crown. In practical terms, a bounty was used to increase the price a farmer could expect. Hemp was to be grown in the colonies by farmers like Washington, and then transported to London where it would be made into sails and ropes for British ships. At the height of the Revolutionary War, the Virginia Assembly would pass its own **hemp bounty**. (Hint: are you beginning to see hemp's importance?)

Hemp history is generally told from the fiber perspective, producing a focus on hemp as a war material. Another history is told by looking at the life-giving aspects of hemp seed, where the focus is on nutrition and the stars are the perfectly balanced Omega fatty acids.

"Washington's Diaries" provide a historical record of his first hemp crop. The diaries read more like a farmer's almanac. These aren't his intimate thoughts. They are grow-notes from a dedicated businessman. His first recorded hemp note in 1765 begins with a May planting:

*May 12-13: "Sowed **Hemp** at Muddy hole by Swamp."*

*May 16: "Sowed **Hemp** at the head of the Meadow at Doeg Run & about Southwards Houses with the Barrel."*

These two farms – Muddy Hole and Doeg Run – were part of the Mount Vernon lands and where Washington planted his hemp crops. There are no hemp entries again until three months later. Washington checks on his plants at Doeg Run and is a bit disappointed …

*August 7: "Began to separate the Male from the Female* **hemp** *at Do—rather too late."*

Here is an informed farmer. Hemp is a sexed plant. This means there are male and female plants. When growing for seed, after pollination of course, the males only limit the growth of the females by competing for sun and soil. That is why the males should have been separated. His annoyance with time – "rather too late" – shows, as we'll see below, that this was his seed patch.

By early September and into October, Washington checks on and harvests his crop of hemp for seed:

*September 4: "Began to Pull the* **Seed Hemp** *but it was not sufficiently ripe."*

*September 25: "***Hempseed** *seems to be in good order for getting – that is of a proper ripeness—but oblige to desist to pull my fodder."*

*October 10: "Finishd pulling* **Seed Hemp** *at River Plantation."*

The harvest is complete. We can glean from the historical record that Washington harvested 5000 pounds of hemp fiber in 1765. There is one more entry for the year regarding **hemp seed**. Washington, while making a note about sowing winter wheat, makes mention of the hemp seed and its harvest:

*October 31: "Finished sowing Wheat in* **Hemp** *Ground at Rivr. Plantn. & plowed in a good deal of shattered* **Hemp Seed—27 Bushls. in all 152.***"*

Washington's first "Hemp Seed" harvest was 152 bushels – quite impressive. He also mentions spreading 27 bushels of "shattered Hemp Seed." If you mill hemp seed you can collect the oil – with the shattered seed being plowed in with the winter wheat as a natural fertilizer. All that seed would have produced a lot of hemp oil – estimated at 80 to 100 gallons. That **superfood-oil** would have been a valuable commodity on a plantation with many needs and feeding hundreds of people.

Now speed forward to 1789-97 and Washington's presidency. POTUS 1 signed a tariff law in 1792 to protect and promote American hemp – which he was growing. He was also still interested in his hemp seed. As POTUS 1 he writes home to Mount Vernon in 1796 with an important hemp question:

> ***"What was done with the Seed saved from the India Hemp last summer?*** *It ought, all of it, to have been sown again; that not only a stock of seed sufficient for my own purposes might have been raised, but to have disseminated the seed to others; as it is **more valuable than the common Hemp**."*

Our presidential hempster was pretty hot for hemp seed – even to the point of disseminating "the seed to others." He also is growing two kinds of hemp from seed – India Hemp and common Hemp. It was the hemp seed, that life-containing seed and its natural goodness, which held Washington's attention throughout his career.

In one of his last letters, a now retired POTUS 1 and farmer again, Washington still had hemp on his mind. On 3 December 1799, he opens a letter with – *"Dear Sir: Have you succeeded, or are you likely to succeed, in procuring the **Hemp seed** I required?"*

This seed would have been required for next year's planting – a season he never saw. Washington died on 14 December, eleven days after the letter, concluding 34 years as a hemp grower. One can say it clearly – he was a hempster to the end.

*Publius*
(2010)

**Search terms**
George Washington's Diaries and hemp; hemp superfood; hemp oil; Omega-3 and Omega-6 EFAs; *Government Grown Polo IL*; Kentucky's 1943 Hemp Seed Project for 4H Clubs; Marc Emery.

**Research and selected readings**
2010: I Brown, et al, *Cannabinoid receptor-dependent and – independent anti-proliferative effects of omega-3ethanolamides in androgen receptor-positive and –negative prostrate cancer cell lines*, Carcinogenesis, September 2010:31(9):1584-91.

2010: A Defilippis, et al, *Omega-3 fatty acids for cardiovascular disease prevention*, Current Treatment Options in Cardiovascular Medicine, August 2010:12(4):365-80.

2009: P Wertz, *Essential fatty acids and dietary stress*, Toxicology and Industrial Health, May-June 2009:25(4-5):279-83.

2005: J Callaway, et al, *Efficacy of dietary hempseed oil in patients with atopic dermatitis (eczema)*, Dermatological Treatment, April 2005:16(2):87-94.

2005: F Silversides and M Lefrancois, *The effect of feeding hemp seed meal to laying hens*, British Poultry Science, April 2005:46(2):231-5.

1985: J Herer, *The Emperor Wears No Clothes*, AH HA Publishing, Van Nuys CA.

1975: R Latta and B Eaton, *Seasonal fluctuations in cannabinoid content of Kansas marijuana*, Economic Botany, April-June 1975:29:153-63.

1735: L Slator, et al, *Instructions for the cultivating and raising of flax and hemp: in a better manner, than that generally practis'd in Ireland*, Printed by Kneeland & Green, Boston MA.

#12

# Spirited place to grow

*A cannabinated reverie*

This is a set and setting piece. I'm having some quiet-spiritual time. Things are to a point where I can hear myself think. Louis Armstrong's *Muggles* is backgrounding softly on vinyl. I'm "cannabinated" – meaning my ECS is actively modulating my consciousness. Retrograde signaling, that form of communication unique to the ECS, is activated. This is a *reverie*, a place where subtle and illuminating thoughts often precede great endeavors.

*Is or Is Not?*
    *Bliss can change one's spirit. No doubt there. The evidence is the bliss. It is a chemical-electrical-synaptic combination. I like how the white-coats named the first endocannabinoid they found, anandamide, after the Sanskrit word for bliss.*
    *Spirit is part of being human. We are not a thing if the spirit is missing. It makes us. If the world was absent spirit, it would be un-animated. World religions contemplate this animation and call it spirituality. This spirituality informs our sense of self. We feel ourselves in the world and it leads us to the earth spirit – we call it Mother Nature or Gaia.*

*Louis Armstrong was spiritual and a cannabinoider. He liked to get all muggled-up. Gotta think cannabinoids helped with his spiritual life.*

*Let's see ... Armstrong had to use his ECS to make music, like all musicians.*

*Guess I can draw the same conclusion regarding love-making ... that an active ECS is part of the energy for sure ...*

*Think of meditation. There is no meditation if you can't control the sense of sound. You can't control your hearing without ECS modulation. No quiet-spiritual time if you can't control noise. In fact, if you can't bring the world into a space of your own – your own internal world of balance – then you live unbalanced.*

*Yogis are cannabinoiders. Yoga demands and facilitates, like all exercise, an active ECS – and yoga is spiritual. It's also easy to see the ECS in Buddha, Tao, the Abrahamic trilogy, Jah Rastafari and Hindu Nirvana. So easy to see, yet ...what keeps people ignorant?*

*This is not a new question, this question of knowing. Parmenides, the pre-Socratic thinker, gave the simplest of answers. The spirit of Truth is found in questioning the evidence of Is and Is Not – that was his answer.*

*The one path, the path of the Is, was shown to him by a Goddess. The other path, the path of the Is Not, the Goddess said "was an inscrutable path."*

*The Goddess said you can't know the Is Not because ... **it Is Not**. She wasn't playing a trick, just showing Parmenides a way of thinking. Her point was you cannot know that which Is Not. She would say "for this cannot be done" – "nor can you express it." The path of Truth is different than the path of Not True – so said the Goddess.*

*The Not True has been the policy of our federal health institutions. Glad to see that's changing. The National Cancer Institute has updated their website to say cannabinoids kill cancer. They even mention apoptosis and how cannabinoids are neuroprotective. It's 2011. The cancer killing benefits of cannabinoids were first noted in 1975. Oh that's the spirit! – And it only took 36 years!*

*Fighting cancer is a fight for forever. It is simply insane to get in the way of people trying to stay alive.* **Cancer is a killer and cannabis is a cancer killer.**

*And yet the beat goes on ... the arrests continue ... cancer keeps winning ... tears at funerals ... sadness for lost ones...*

*I often feel tears of joy when my ECS is active. Yeah, I feel that a lot. Crying is most definitely spiritual. I cry a lot when high. Activating the ECS allows emotions to come into play. It is that retrograde signaling moment that humans know so well – yet don't know it's called retrograde signaling. Those times when we hear-feel-see-taste-and-smell our consciousness. Some emotions pass on forever. Some get thought about forever. Retrograde signaling allows me to think things over, to ponder, speculate and wonder – wow – can't imagine a world without wonder ...*

*Chewing the cud, reflecting, sorting, thinking, remembering, learning, creating ... these are part of spirit-management and homeostasis ... we'd be all un-balanced without 'em, yet they all depend on the ECS ... then why ...*

*Wait ...the Goddess warned Parmenides about such thinking. An inscrutable path she called it ... "Don't go that way!" she would warn.*

*If you focus on the ECS as an Is Not, that would be the inscrutable path the Goddess mentioned. It's like trying to take a pathway that doesn't exist.*

*The ECS is an Is. ...Whoa ... taking the pathway that doesn't exist. There would be evil things on an inscrutable path. Perhaps even a big Evil Lie lying on such a pathway. It would block the way of Truth – of the Is.*

*A lie that Big would have to be really powerful and filled with deceit ...something really awful ...really ...*

*Wait ... I'm having one of those ideas ...*

*Publius*
(2011)

**Search terms**
Louis Armstrong's *Muggles*; Bob Marley; ECS stress adaptation; bliss and hypothalamic-pituitary-adrenal axis; Genesis 1-11; Scythians; apoptosis; Parmenides; retrograde signaling; National Cancer Institute's *Cannabis and Cannabinoids*.

**Research and selected readings**
2011: **National Cancer Institute**, a component of the US National Institutes of Health, *Cannabis and Cannabinoids*, cancer.gov. (*See 1975 entry on next page from the National Cancer Institute.*)

2011: T Brock, *Cannabinoid signaling: the original retrograde signaling pathway*, Cayman Chemical online.

2011: P Kvillemo and R Branstrom, *Experiences of a mindfulness-based stress-reduction [yoga] intervention among cancer patients*, Cancer Nursing, Jan-Feb 2011:34(1):24-31.

2010: V Aloyo, et al, *Inverse agonism at serotonin and cannabinoid receptors*, Progress in Molecular Biology and Translational Science, 2010:91:1-40.

2010: M Hill, et al, *Endogenous cannabinoid signaling is essential for stress adaptation*, Proceedings of the National Academy of Sciences USA, May 2010:107(20):9406-11.

2010: M Hill, et al, *Endogenous cannabinoid signaling is required for voluntary exercise-induced enhancement of progenitor cell proliferation in the hippocampus*, Hippocampus, April 2010:20(4):513-23.

2009: Z Mouslech and V Valla, *Endocannabinoid system: an overview of its potential in current medical practice*, Neuro Endocrinology Letters, 2009:30(2):153-79.

2008: I Racz, et al, *Anandamide effects on 5-HT(3) receptors in vivo*, European Journal of Pharmacology, October 2008:596(1-3):98-101.

2006: P Safo, et al, *Retrograde endocannabinoid signaling in the cerebellar cortex*, Cerebellum, 2006:5(2):134-45.

2006: D Osei-Hyiaman, et al, *The role of the endocannabinoid system in the control of energy homeostasis*, International Journal of Obesity, April 2006:30 Suppl 1:S33-8.

2004: A Herman, *The illustrated to think like God: Pythagoras and Parmenides, the origins of philosophy*, Parmenides Publishing, Las Vegas NV.

2000 [1996]: J Bello, *The benefits of marijuana: physical, psychological & spiritual*, Lifeservices Press, Susquehanna PA.

1990 [1946]: M Mezzrow and B Wolfe, *Really the Blues*, Citadel Underground Edition, New York NY.

1979: P Morahan, et al, *Effects of cannabinoids on host resistance to Listeria monocytogenes and herpes simplex virus*, Infection and Immunity, March 1979:23(3):670-4.

1978: S Smith, et al, *Structure-activity relationships of natural and synthetic cannabinoids in suppression of humoral and cell-mediated immunity*, Pharmacology and Experimental Therapeutics, October 1978:207(1):165-70.

1975: A Munson, et al, *Antineoplastic [anticancer] activity of cannabinoids*, Journal of the **National Cancer Institute**, September 1975:55(3):597-602.

# Part Two: Liberty

*Liberty* lies in the hearts of men and women; when *it* dies there, no constitution, no law, no court, can save *it*; no constitution, no law, no court can even do much to help *it*.

Justice Learned Hand (1872-1961)

#13

# Liberty to change Nixon's law

*"For all these reasons, we reject the total prohibition approach and its variations."*

We agree with the above quote – although it's not from us. The quote is from 1972 and the only presidential report on cannabis – *The National Commission on Marihuana and Drug Abuse.*

The war on cannabis has had two distinct federal laws. First there was the 1937 Marihuana Tax Act, which was ruled unconstitutional by the Supremes in *Leary vs. U.S. (1969).* This means for 32 years people were unconstitutionally prosecuted, convicted and incarcerated.

Into this vacuum was sucked Nixon's contribution to 21$^{st}$ century cannabis policy – the 1970 Comprehensive Drug Abuse Prevention and Control Act. This law contains the Controlled Substances Act (CSA) making cannabis Schedule 1. This means in *Bizarro World* herbal cannabinoids have no medical value and 40 more years of prosecution, conviction and incarceration.

Nixon is history and yet his tricky law lives on – though one can predict not much longer. That is because of the ECS. The ECS is not political: it is a fact of biology. It is now only a matter of time until the biological ECS upends the political CSA in a way that even a bureaucrat can understand. The cannabis conflict has morphed into a matter of *will* – the willfully ignorant and the willingly scientific.

Willful ignorance had a great friend in POTUS 37 Nixon. One can see this ignorance in his willingness to politicize cannabis use. Listen to Nixon's voice on the infamous tapes and hear how he hated the Jews, the hippies, the blacks and marijuana. Nixon was good at hating.

In March 1972, Nixon was presented with the commission's conclusions. The recommendations were rejected. It was the year of Nixon's re-election and two years before his disgraceful resignation.

The commission's report, *Marihuana: A Signal of Misunderstanding*, is remarkable for its clarity. As compared to alcohol prohibition, the report noted that from 1937-69 the federal government had aimed to eliminate the use of marijuana. This was done by utilizing a policy "***far more comprehensive than the restrictions established during the prohibition of alcohol.***" It was still legal to possess and consume alcohol during its prohibition. What was forbidden by constitutional amendment was the "manufacturing" of alcohol.

During the 37-69 phase, the elimination of the plant was pursued through a get-tough punishment model. The commission noted penalties for cannabis possession were made heavier and heavier. First-time possession was a felony in every jurisdiction and a second offense generally carried a mandatory sentence. The commission noted that society was moving away from a zero-tolerance model toward a more reasonable and humane policy – a form of decriminalization.

Nixon's response was the exact opposite. He furthered the cause of total cannabinoid prohibition by defining cannabis as a Schedule 1 controlled substance. A Schedule 1 drug is supposed to have no medicinal value: in the grand hypocritical tradition, in 2003 the US government received a patent on cannabinoids as antioxidants and neuroprotectants, US patent #6,630,507. Obviously, something is wrong.

In 2010 federal law is still a total prohibition law – just like Nixon wanted. His commission defined total prohibition as when "***all marihuana-related behavior, including possession for personal use within the home, is prohibited by criminal law.***"

Today this policy lives on with over 800,000 cannabinoiders annually arrested for cannabis possession.

It really is that strange in *Bizarro World*. Nixon and Congress not only ignored the commission's recommendations – they actually did what the commission said **not** to do. The report spelled out three points against total cannabis prohibition – all of which have become our reality! The report found that total cannabis prohibition was ***Philosophically Inappropriate, Constitutionally Suspect and Functionally Inappropriate***:

- ***Philosophically Inappropriate*** because cannabis prohibition undermined privacy: *"The actual and potential harm of use of the drug [i.e., cannabinoids] is not great enough to justify intrusion by the criminal law into private behavior."*

- ***Constitutionally Suspect*** because cannabis prohibition is opposed to a free society and the provisions of the Bill of Rights. The report identified the Fourth Amendment as *"reflecting a constitutional commitment to the value of individual privacy."* Quoting from Olmstead vs. U.S. (1928), the commission noted that *"the right to be let alone"* is *"the most comprehensive of rights and the right most valued by civilized men."*

- ***Functionally Inappropriate*** because cannabis prohibition does nothing to stop supply: *"prohibiting possession for personal use has no substantive relation to interdicting supply."*

That's a lot of clarity. One would think Jon Stewart could have a bit of fun with this. He could start by showing the cannabis using sons of POTUS 38 and POTUS 39, a weedable Governor Reagan, a smoking Quayle and Gore, an edible-eating POTUS 42, a frat-party puffin' POTUS 43, and a 1975 "see through all the hypocrisy and bullshit and cheap moralism" POTUS 44. The commission warned against such folly: ***"the possession offense is of little functional benefit to the discouragement policy and carries heavy social costs, not the least of which is disrespect and cynicism among some of the young."***

Cue Stewart's trademark look of exasperation and *this ain't funny but I better laugh because it hurts* moment.

The commission's cover letter closed with a message of **hope**:

*"We **hope** this Report will be a foundation upon which credibility in this area can be restored and upon which a rational policy can be predicated."*

Beyond hope is action. It's time to end Nixon's infamous legacy of lies, trickery and ignorance.

*Publius*
(2010)

### Search terms
Shafer Commission; PubMed hypothalamic-pituitary-adrenocortical (HPA axis) and cannabinoids; POTUS cannabis use; Timothy Leary; Controlled Substances Act; Nixon's marijuana tapes; Law Enforcement Against Prohibition (LEAP).

### Research and selected readings
2010: M Hill and B McEwen, *Involvement of the endocannabinoid system in the neurobehavioral effects of stress and glucocorticoids*, Progress in Neuro-psychopharmacology & Biological Psychiatry, June 2010:34(5):791-7.

2008: M Steiner and C Wotjak, *Role of the endocannabinoid system in regulation of the hypothalamic-pituitary-adrenocortical axis*, Progress in Brain Research, 2008:170:397-432.

2008: V Haller, et al, *Modulation of opioids via protection of anandamide degradation by fatty acid amide hydrolase*, European Journal of Pharmacology, December 2008:600(1-3):50-8.

2007: D Cota, et al, *Requirement of cannabinoid receptor type 1 for the basal modulation of hypothalamic-pituitary-adrenocortical axis function*, Endocrinology, April 2007:148(4):1574-81.

2004: I Barna, et al, *The role of endogenous cannabinoids in the hypothalamic-pituitary-adrenocortical axis regulation: in vivo and in vitro studies in CB1 receptor knockout mice*, Life Sciences, October 2004:75(24):2959-70.

2003: M Booth, *Cannabis – a history*, Picador: St. Martin's Press, New York NY.

2003: G Stefano, et al, *Endocannabinoids as autoregulatory signaling molecules: coupling to nitric oxide and a possible association with the relaxation response*, Medical Science Monitor, April 2003:9(4):RA63-75.

2002: J Wiley and B Martin, *Cannabinoid pharmacology: implications for additional cannabinoid receptor subtypes*, Chemistry and Physics of Lipids, December 2002:121(1-2):57-63.

2000: G Stefano, et al, *2-arachidonoyl-gylcerol (2-AG) stimulates nitric oxide release from human immune and vascular tissues and invertebrate immunocytes by cannabinoid receptor 1*, Pharmacological Research, October 2000:42(4):317-22.

1999 [1974]: R Bonnie and C Whitebread, *The marijuana conviction: a history of marijuana prohibition in the United States*, The Lindesmith Center, New York NY.

#14

## Intermission – let's get high

*Let's take a look at "**high**" ~*

> **High** *seas: The word "**high**" is used to indicate that the seas are public, just as "**high**way" means a "public way." In both cases, of course, "**high**" also means "chief" or "principal."*

Why Do We Say It?

**High** road
**High** hopes
**High** times
**Higher** forms of life
**Highest** potential

> **High**-*minded: adjective – being on a **high** intellectual or moral level. Characterized by elevated ideals or conduct; noble.*

**High** importance
**Higher** learning
**Higher** education

**High** endurance
**Higher** ground

> *"And if the **high** didn't solve whatever it was that was getting you down, **it** could at least help you laugh at the world's ongoing folly and see through all the hypocrisy and bullshit and cheap moralism."*

Barack Obama, *Dreams from My Father*, 1996

**High** expectations
**High** resolution
**High** court
**High** stakes
**High** anxiety
**High** official – as in eminent in rank or status

> *"With all the things we've got to worry about, and our Justice Department should be doing, that [federal raids on medical cannabis patients] probably shouldn't be a **high** priority."*

Senator Obama, 2007

**High** scores
**High** roller
**High** jump
**High** energy
**High** quality

> *"**High** is determined by low."*

Tao Te Ching

**High** pitch
**High** note

**High** turnout
**High** confidence
**High** standards

*"I'd been getting bored with the stereotyped changes (harmonies) that were being used all the time . . . I found that by using the **higher** intervals of a chord as a melody line and backing them with appropriately related changes, I could play the thing I'd been hearing. I came alive."*

Charlie Parker

**High** summer
**High** beam
**High** point
**High** speed
**High** mileage
**High** tourist season

*The Acropolis = **high** + "polis" = city: the upper, fortified part of an ancient city, "the **high** city": the most famous and important part of Athens.*

**High** horse
**High** net worth
**High** income
**High** maintenance
**High** fidelity
**Higher** power

*Thus saith the Lord:*
*Ye are gods and children of the Most **High**.*

Psalm 82

**High** spirits
**High**lighting
**High** noon
**High** jinx
**High** life
**High** moral ground

> *A **High** Place: The word "altar" derives from the Latin altare, meaning a "**high** place." In the great religious traditions of the East, the altar similarly assumes a central role in focusing the mind towards the "**high** place" where the enlightened qualities of the deities shine forth.*

Tibetan Buddhist Altars

The Helper's **High** – named for the good feeling that follows helping others.

*"What does '**high**' mean to you, your **high**ness?"*

*Publius*
(2010)

**Search terms**
*High Times*; DSI and DSE; retrograde signaling and ECS; anandamide, 2-AG and entourage effect; runner's high and endocannabinoids; cannabis arrests; Keith Stroup.

**Research and selected readings**
2010: J Fuss and P Gass, *Endocannabinoids and voluntary activity in mice: runner's high and long-term consequences in emotional behaviors*, Experimental Neurology, July 2010:224(1):103-5.

2009: R Grim, *This is your country on drugs: the secret history of getting high in America*, John Wiley & Sons, Hoboken NJ.

2009: D Sagar, et al, *Dynamic regulation of the endocannabinoid system: implications for analgesia*, Molecular Pain, October 2009:5:59.

2008: J Gertsch, *Immunomodulatory lipids in plants: plant fatty acid amides and the human endocannabinoid system*, Planta Medica, May 2008:74(6):638-50.

2007: S Alexander and D Kendall, *The complications of promiscuity: endocannabinoid action and metabolism*, British Journal of Pharmacology, November 2007:152(5):602-23.

2007: S O'Sullivan, *Cannabinoids go nuclear: evidence for activation of peroxisome proliferator-activated receptors*, British Journal of Pharmacology, November 2007:152(5):576-82.

2004: A Howlett, et al, *Cannabinoid physiology and pharmacology: 30 years of progress*, Neuropharmacology, 2004:47 Suppl 1:345-58.

2000: S Young, *Maximizing harm: losers and winners in the drug war*, Writer's Showcase (iUniverse.com), Bloomington IN.

1998: S Ben-Shabat, et al, *An entourage effect: inactive endogenous fatty acid glycerol esters enhance 2-arachidonoyl-glycerol cannabinoid activity*, European Journal of Pharmacology, July 1998:353(1):23-31.

1998: M Randall and D Kendall, *Endocannabinoids: a new class of vasoactive substances*, Trends in Pharmacological Sciences, February 1998:19(2):55-8.

Mother Cannabis
INSANE LAWS

#15

# The birth of the ECS

Which came first, the chicken or the egg?

A cell mutation occurred about 550 million years ago marking the emergence of animals with bones. This split also marks the birth of the ECS. A 2009 NY Academy of Sciences paper put it this way: *"Indeed the endocannabinoid system is a **very ancient signaling system**, being clearly present from the divergence of the protostomian/deuterostomian."*

This divergence is the genetic marker between non-vertebrate and vertebrate species. Vertebrate reproduction is unimaginable without the **egg**. The proto/deutero split created cells that make eggs. Without this division there would be no chicken – which makes egg the answer.

Even though proof of the ECS exists in the fossil evidence, the Illinois General Assembly is still acting like a protostomian (spineless). I'm a veteran of the medical cannabis war in Illinois. I've seen how the system works: consciousness-raising, organizing, financing, testifying, debating, mediating and counting the final votes. All in the effort to show what seems obvious – that this is not just about cannabis. This battle has also demonstrated *that the right to self-medicate is the same as the right to self-defense*.

Dr. Benjamin Rush was a founder of our country, colleague of George Washington, and namesake of Chicago's Rush University Medical Center. As a revolutionary he advocated for the constitutional protection of medical freedom. He was blunt: *"Unless we put **Medical Freedom** into the Constitution, the time will come when medicine will organize into an undercover dictatorship."*

Of course that sounds awful – "an undercover dictatorship." The exact words "Medical Freedom" did not make it into our Constitution as Rush wanted. Nonetheless, the idea is there in concept and principle. The right to self-defense is a principle and it logically includes defending one's health. Citizens empowered to recognize new information regarding their wellness and able to act accordingly – that sounds like a working definition for **medical freedom** to me.

More recently, Dennis Peron advocated for the 1996 citizen's initiative allowing medical cannabis in California. Peron is credited with the bumper-sticker worthy quote *"All cannabis use is medical."* His point accurately presents cannabinoids as therapeutic and points to the ECS's role in biology and the development of vertebrate life.

If all use is medical, meaning that herbal ECS supplementation has wellness aspects, then we should find supporting evidence in the science of human reproduction – and we do. A 2002 research paper noted these facts concerning the ECS: ***"Cannabinoid receptors and/or AEA [anandamide] are present in mammalian reproductive organs including the testis, epididymis [sperm storage], prostate, ovary, uterus, sperm, preimplantation embryo and placenta, as well as prostatic and mammary carcinomas."***

Another study in 2002 found **anandamide** in the following "reproductive fluids": human seminal plasma and mid-cycle oviductal and follicular fluids. And in case there is any doubt that the ECS plays a principal role in pregnancy, the same study reported: ***"Sperm are sequentially exposed to these reproductive fluids as they move from the vagina to the site of fertilization."***

Well? … All the way to the site of fertilization … that seems to be the moment of … conception.

Clearly by 2002 the scientific community knew of a connection between the ECS and pregnancy. Jump to 2010 and the work of a British Endocannabinoid Research Group. These white-coats used *"a rapid, highly sensitive, specific and highly reproducible ultra-*

*high-performance liquid chromatography-tandem mass spectrometry method"* for the analysis of compounds that support the ECS. They found anandamide and **"entourage compounds"** in human bio-fluids including plasma, serum, breast milk and amniotic fluids.

Entourage compounds create an **"entourage effect"** and support the ECS without (always) activating cannabinoid receptors. The entourage effect acts by modulating the metabolism of cannabinoids, preventing them from leaving the active system. These compounds have unfamiliar and not easily pronounceable names like **palmitoylethanolamide** (PEA) and **oleoylethanolamide** (OEA) – but you probably can't get pregnant without them.

With its vital role in pregnancy established, it's apparent that a malfunctioning or deficient ECS would be bad. ***Hyperemesis gravidarum (HG)*** is an apt example. Pregnancy involves some nausea and vomiting. With HG, these conditions become pernicious and life-threatening for mother and fetus. In *Women and cannabis: medicine, science, and sociology*, there are testimonials from HG diagnosed women who supplemented with herbal cannabinoids – stories of effectiveness in alleviating the pernicious nausea and vomiting. Hearing their words I realized they were only defending themselves and the life inside them. Now I saw them as individuals using cannabinoids in **self-defense** and **self-preservation** – defending and preserving life.

Testimonials aren't policy. Most state and federal laws work to keep citizen's <u>from</u> ECS supplementation – yet the scientific evidence points <u>toward</u> supplementation. Someone today seeking to become pregnant – how could they ignore the evidence? How can we?

*Publius*
*(2010)*

**Search terms**
ECS entourage compounds and effect; ECS and the protostomian/deuterostomian divergence; hyperemesis gravidarum; anandamide; N-acylethanolamides; Dr. Benjamin Rush; Dennis Peron.

**Research and selected readings**
2011: D Fraga, et al, *Cannabinoids inhibit migration of microglial-like cells to the HIV protein Tat*, Neuroimmune Pharmacology, 7 July 2011 [Epub].

2010: P Lam, et al, *Simultaneous measurement of three N-acylethanolamides in human bio-matrices using ultra performance lipid chromatography-tandem mass spectrometry*, Analytical and Bioanalytical Chemistry, November 2010:398(5):2089-97.

2010: A El Albini, et al, *Large colonial organisms with coordinated growth in oxygenated environments 2.1 Gyr ago*, Nature, July 2010:466(7302):100-4.

2010: J Jueckstock, et al, *Managing hyperemesis gravidarum: a multimodal challenge*, BMC Medicine, July 2010:15(8):46.

2010: A Taylor, et al, *Endocannabinoids and pregnancy*, Clinica Chimica Acta: International Journal of Clinical Chemistry, July 2010:411(13-14):921-30.

2010: E Raborn and G Cabral, *Cannabinoid inhibition of macrophage migration to the trans-activating (Tat) protein of HIV-1 is linked to the CB(2) cannabinoid receptor*, Pharmacology and Experimental Therapeutics, April 2010:333(1):319-27.

2009: P Grimaldi, et al, *The endocannabinoid system and pivotal role of the CB2 receptor in mouse spermatogenesis*, Proceedings of the National Academy of Sciences USA, July 2009:106(27):11131-6.

2009: S Fasano, et al, *The endocannabinoid system: an ancient signaling involved in the control of male fertility*, NY Academy of Sciences, April 2009:1163:112-24.

2008: T Stincic and R Hyson, *Localization of CB1 receptor mRNA in the brain of chicks (Gallus domesticus)*, Brain Research, December 2008:1245:61-73.

2008: M Maccarrone, *CB2 receptors in reproduction*, British Journal of Pharmacology, January 2008:153(2):189-98.

2006: M Maccarrone, et al, *Regulation by cannabinoid receptors of anandamide transport across the blood-brain barrier and through other endothelial cells*, Thrombosis and Haemostasis, January 2006:95(1):117-27.

2005: M Elphick and M Egertova, *The phylogenetic distribution and evolutionary origins of endocannabinoid signaling*, Handbook of Experimental Pharmacology, 2005:168:283-297.

2002: Edited by E Russo, et al, *Women and cannabis: medicine, science, and sociology*, Haworth Press: New York NY: co-published as the Journal of Cannabis Therapeutics, 2002:2(3-4).

2002: H Schuel, et al, *N-Acylethanolamines in human reproductive fluids*, Chemistry and Physics of Lipids, December 2002:121(1-2):211-27.

2001: M Elphick and M Egertova, *The neurobiology and evolution of cannabinoid signaling*, Philosophical Transactions of the Royal Society of London, March 2001:356(1407):381-408.

#16

# Safe is safe, *Per se*: driving and cannabinoids

> *That range has not been shown to extend into the area that can rightfully be regarded as dangerous or an obviously unacceptable threat to public safety.*
>
> US DOT (1999) concerning cannabis and driving

**Publius:** You know, by definition, the three of us are ***impaired*** right now.

**Mary Jane:** You shouldn't be driving then …

**Publius:** I'm not joking. We ate cannabis last evening and I'm driving. By definition, under *"Per se"* laws, I'm impaired and so are you two.

**Ananda:** He's right. Illinois is a *Per se* state and Obama wants it to be a federal law.

*Per se* laws mean you don't have to show impairment. You are guilty by association. If they find the metabolite THC-COOH in your urine, you are guilty of driving under the influence of drugs.

**Publius:** … And it's only cannabis-COOHs. If a pharmaceutical company makes the cannabinoid, like Marinol, then it's a get out of jail free card.

**Mary Jane:** What about pharmaceuticals in general – do they get a pass?

**Ananda:** They do. Take that ABILIFY ad you showed me from the magazine – checkout the risks and see what it says about driving.

**Mary Jane:** Okay, here it is: *"Other risks may include lightheadedness upon standing, seizures, trouble swallowing, or **impairment in judgment** or motor skills. Until you know how ABILIFY affects you, you should not drive or operate machinery."*
Wow – that means they leave it up to the individual to judge for themselves if they are impaired, even though they just said *ABILIFY may impair judgment!*

**Publius:** I know. With cannabis, we are guilty all the time – no room for our own judgment.

**Mary Jane:** Loony.

**Ananda:** When you read that, you said "other risks" – what are they?

**Mary Jane:** Okay, let's see … there are lots.
There are three bulleted warnings about really bad things. There's *neuroleptic malignant syndrome*, a rare but potentially fatal condition; *tardive dyskinesia*, which is the risk of abnormal or uncontrollable facial movements, which may become permanent; and *high blood sugar*, which can lead to coma or death.

**Ananda:** Or death, huh …

**Mary Jane:** Yeah – coma or death.

**Publius:** What else?

**Mary Jane:** There's a summary of common side effects that 10 percent or more adults experience. It lists *"nausea, vomiting, constipation, headache, dizziness, an inner sense of restlessness or need to move, anxiety and insomnia."* Then it closes with an alcohol warning: *"You should avoid alcohol while taking ABILIFY."*

**Ananda:** What is this drug? Who takes it?

**Mary Jane:** ABILIFY is an antipsychotic and it is used as a second antidepressant. The ad says it's prescribed for *"unresolved symptoms of depression."* Seems you take it when a drug such as Prozac or Zoloft isn't resolving your depression.

**Ananda:** *So they double-down on depression with an antipsychotic?*

**Publius:** Yes. ABILIFY is one of the top five selling pharmaceuticals in a $300 billion dollar industry.

**Ananda:** They have a different view of this in Europe. Chris Berg, the Chicago painter, tells a story about a drive he and his friends took in Amsterdam. In Holland they have a zero-tolerance policy to prevent drunk drivers from hurting people. They are vigilant and use roadblocks to catch drinkers. For a first offense you get thrown in jail and lose your license for a few years.

So Chris and his friends were on their way to town and had just smoked a spliff – which is a mix of tobacco and cannabis – and out of the blue there was a roadblock. They pulled over to the inspection area, rolled down the windows and smoke flowed out of the car – just like in the movies. The police officer came up to the car and looked in and asked, *"Have you been drinking?"*

The driver said, *"No, I'm high – do I look drunk?"*

At that time the officer laughed and said *"Okay, fine. I had to ask though. You know we don't mind people smoking cause it makes them drive more cautiously and slower. It's the drinking that's the problem. Have a nice night."*

**Publius:** You say this happened on Mars?

**Ananda:** No, Holland.

**Publius:** That thing about slowing down and being more cautious has some science support. The US Department of Transportation did two studies in Holland during the 90s. Look there on the clipboard, the 1999 one …

**Mary Jane:** Got it.

**Publius:** Check out the highlighted lines from the general results.

**Mary Jane:** Okay, here it is: ***"That range has not been shown to extend into the area that can rightfully be regarded as dangerous or an obviously unacceptable threat to public safety."***

**Ananda:** Are they talking about pot?

**Publius:** Yes they are: THC to be specific.
Read the next sentence as well.

**Mary Jane:** All right: ***"Alcohol** present in blood concentrations around the legal limit (0.10 g/dl) in most American states **is more impairing than anything subjects have shown after THC alone in our studies.***"

**Ananda:** No way! – And that's from the 90s?

**Publius:** Yes. It's also an example of *an absence having a presence:* if they had negative science about cannabinoids and driving, we would have seen the drugged driving commercials by now.

**Ananda:** What was the first line again?

**Mary Jane:** Sure – that THC and driving cannot be *"rightfully regarded as dangerous or an obviously unacceptable threat to public safety."*

**Publius:** Of course no one has ever heard of this federal research.

**Ananda:** That's not an accident … with today's simulators this would be easy to test.

**Mary Jane:** That's true.

**Ananda:** While they're at it they can test the pharmaceuticals – safe is safe, right? Let's test some combinations like Prozac/Zoloft with ABILIFY and see how they do.

**Mary Jane:** Good one! You think like a scientist.

**Ananda:** Nice.
Oh, here we are. Thanks for the lift and I'll see ya later!

**Publius/Mary Jane:** See ya!

*Publius*
*(2011)*

### Search terms
ABILIFY; federal *Per se* driving laws; THC-COOH; ECS and driving; alcohol and driving; *DOT HS 808 939 (1999)*; *DOT HS 808 078 (1993)*; Allen St. Pierre.

### Research and selected readings
2011: Chicago Tribune, *Most popular drugs in America and how much we spend on medications*, 21 April 2011.

2010: L Orriols, et al, *Prescription medicines and the risk of road traffic crashes: a French registry-based study*, PLoS Medicine, November 2010:7(11):e1000366.

2010: P Armentano, *DUID Legislation: what it means, who's behind it, and strategies to prevent it*, NORML/NORML Foundation, 11 October 2010.

2010: B Smink, et al, *The relationship between benzodiazepine use and traffic accidents: A systematic literature review*, CNS Drugs, August 2010:24(8):639-53.

2010: R DuPont, *Prescription drug abuse: an epidemic dilemma*, Psychoactive Drugs, June 2010:42(2):127-32.

2010: J Sullum, *Smoke a joint, get arrested for drugged driving a week later*, Reason, 13 May 2010.

2006: J Sullum, *Impaired reasoning: should last week's joint disqualify a pot smoker from driving today?* Reason, 28 June 2006.

2003: P Sparling, et al, *Exercise activates the endocannabinoid system*, NeuroReport, December 2003:14(17):2209-11.

1999: W Hindrik, et al, *Marijuana, alcohol, and actual driving performance*, DOT HS 808 939, National Traffic Safety Administration, US Department of Transportation, Washington DC.

1993: J Robbe and J O'Hanlon, *Marijuana and actual driving performance*, DOT HS 808 078, National Highway Traffic Safety Administration, US Department of Transportation, Washington DC.

1969: A Crancer, et al, *Comparison of the effects of marihuana and alcohol on simulated driving performance*, Science, May 1969:164(881):851-4.

#17

## Ownership rights – FOID meets COID

*Owners of guns must use them responsibly: the same goes for cannabis owners. In Illinois, a citizen of any age that owns a gun must pay a $10 fee to apply for a Firearm Owner's Identification (FOID) card. Publius, as a citizen owning cannabis, would gladly pay a $10 fee to apply for a Cannabis Owner's Identification (COID) card.*

I'm happy for Illinois resident Bubba Ludwig. He has been given a family gift to treasure for the rest of his life. His grandfather, an avid trap shooter, bought and gave his grandson a 12-gauge shotgun. The father, upon hearing the news of grandpa's gift, took the next appropriate steps to exercise Bubba's Second Amendment right.

Mr. Ludwig printed out the FOID card application available on the Illinois State Police website. This is our state's way of regulating a constitutionally protected right – the right to bear arms. In this case, the father had to fill out the application because his son was only 10 months old. Yes, 10 months old. The youngster was unable to sign his name so the father simply placed a pen in Bubba's hand and let him scribble something unique.

The typical-looking state ID card soon arrived in the mail. Bubba's FOID card displays a picture of the grinning toothless baby next to some personal information – such as his height of 27 inches and weight of 20 pounds. Even though (apparently) this young citizen cannot use the 12-gauge shotgun, his right to own the gun (and ammunition) is protected in Illinois. One can almost imagine the little tyke legally transporting his unloaded weapon to the sandbox.

In Illinois, an individual can get a permit to drive a car at 15, get married at 16 (with parental consent), join the military at 17 (with parental consent), vote in elections at 18, and at the age of 21 be declared responsible enough to drink alcohol. So when is the cannabis age? 20? 40? 60? 80? . . . When?

As a FOID card holder, I understand and appreciate the Second Amendment right to own a gun. I understand the amendment as a protection of my right to self-preservation – to defend myself. Herbal cannabinoids are the same thing, a tool of self-preservation, and their use should be **protected not prosecuted**.

"Protected?" you ask.

Yes. Cannabinoids and the ECS modulate the human body – meaning they modulate life, liberty and the pursuit of happiness. In Illinois, these are the first rights protected. Here are the words from the Illinois Constitution, Section 1 of the Bill of Rights:

*"All men are by nature free and independent and have **certain inherent and inalienable rights** among which are **life, liberty and the pursuit of happiness.**"*

It's worth recalling, given our current political times, why we have words like these and what they are supposed to mean. Perhaps they're there for more than history lessons and feel good sloganeering. Perhaps they are there to help us.

This is an easy solution for states like Illinois that don't have a system in place for protecting medical cannabis patients. Card identification systems have already been implemented in the 14 medical states. But stop for a moment. The COID card is more than a medical card. Think of this example: no one is asked to wait for a FOID card until they are under attack. No one says you have to wait until you are attacked before you can possess a gun. That would be silly. The COID card system should be thought of in the same manner. We have to move beyond the "are you sick enough for cannabinoids?" way of thinking. It would be wrong to ask gun owners "are you under attack enough for your right to bear arms?" Rights don't function that way.

The ECS is a tool used by our bodies to modulate the pressures of the every day. It has evolved with us to help us. Just like cannabinoids and the ECS, the COID card is for everyone. The FOID card is the regulatory moment of the right to defend my biology; the COID card is the equivalent defended right in herbal form.

And it is about rights. In Illinois, there's no age limit or qualifying examination for gun owners. That is fine; I would just like the same rights for cannabis owners.

What needs to be discussed is how my right to self-preservation **excludes** the right to cultivate and consume herbal cannabinoids – and yet an infant's right to own a gun is protected.

Clearly, this book tells of a reality where cannabinoids and the ECS are fundamental to life, liberty and the pursuit of happiness. To be explicit for a moment, we're talking about saving lives – as in cannabinoids modulate the depression that often accompanies illness and life. Suicide is too often a consideration and consequence of pain and suffering. This can be helped. A search on PubMed shows that herbal cannabinoids and the ECS modulate depression and suicidal thoughts. So where is the card protecting my right to self-preservation? Where's my COID card protecting my right to grow, possess and consume life-preserving herbal cannabinoids?

On the application for the Illinois FOID card, there is no qualifying gun test, required doctor's evaluation, or licensed training class needed to apply for a FOID card. The owners of herbal cannabinoids deserve the same liberty – as the founders and our ideals reveal.

*Approval from the government to own a plant* – that sounds silly, doesn't it? It wouldn't sound silly to the 40,000 Illinois citizens arrested annually for pot, nor would it sound silly to the 800,000 national arrests for herbal cannabinoids. Though it's easy to predict those hundreds-of-thousands would pay the $10 fee with a silly smile on their face – just like the one that would be on their COID card.

*Publius*
(2010)

### Search terms
US Constitution, Second Amendment; IL Constitution, Section 1 of the Bill of Rights; Illinois FOID; Bubba Ludwig FOID; PubMed cannabinoids antidepressant.

### Research and selected readings
2010: A El-Alfy, et al, *Antidepressant-like effect of delta9-tetrahydrocannabinol and other cannabinoids isolated from Cannabis sativa L.,* Pharmacology, Biochemistry, and Behavior, June 2010:95(4):434-42.

2010: C Chiu, et al, *Dopaminergic modulation of endocannabinoid-mediated plasticity at GABAergic synapses in the prefrontal cortex,* Neuroscience, May 2010:30(21):7236-48.

2010: T Lerner, et al, *Endocannabinoid signaling mediates psychomotor activation by adenosine A2A antagonists,* Neuroscience, February 2010:30(6):2160-4.

2010: T Zanelati, et al, *Antidepressant-like effects of cannabidiol in mice: possible involvement of 5-HT1A receptors,* British Journal of Pharmacology, January 2010:159(1):122-8.

2009: M Urbanski, et al, *Depolarizing GABAergic synaptic input triggers endocannabinoid-mediated retrograde synaptic signaling,* Synapse, August 2009:63(8):643-52.

2009: M Kano, et al, *Endocannabinoid-mediated control of synaptic transmission,* Physiological Review, January 2009:89(1):309-80.

2005: W Jiang, et al, *Cannabinoids promote embryonic and adult hippocampus neurogenesis and produce anxiolytic- and antidepressant-like effects*, Clinical Investigation, November 2005:115(11):3104-16.

2003: A Colin, et al, *Lipids, depression and suicide*, Encephale, Jan-Feb 2003:29(1):49-58.

1998: D Piomelli, et al, *Endogenous cannabinoid signaling*, Neurobiology of Disease, December 1998:5(6 Pt B):462-73.

---

**Fatty Acids**

A chemical molecule consisting of carbon and hydrogen atoms bonded in a chainlike structure; combined through its acid group (-COOH) with the alcohol glycerol to form triglycerides. They are carboxylic acids with long hydrocarbon side chains that may or may not contain carbon double bonds. Most naturally occurring fatty acids have an even number of carbon atoms because they are synthesized from 2-carbon units. Fatty acids rarely have less than 14 or more than 20 carbon atoms in biological systems.

Fatty acids are rarely "free." They most frequently occur as esterified components of other saponifiable lipids. Some fatty acids are essential, that is, our bodies cannot make them, therefore we have to eat them. Two essential fatty acids in humans are linoleic and linolenic acid.

*Butter through the Ages*

---

\#18

# Publius and CooH Meetup

*THC, a marker called CooH, **and our fat***

**Publius:** Hi – is that you?

**CooH:** Yeah – you Publius?

**Publius:** Right – nice meeting you.

**CooH:** You too. I like how you can do this …

**Publius:** What do you mean?

**CooH:** Well, I'm an acidic marker and you're a penname – and we're meeting up in a coffeehouse – it's like not real and real.

**Publius:** I know …
I looked you up and brought a picture.

**CooH:** You brought a picture?

**Publius:** Yeah. Here's you on my phone:

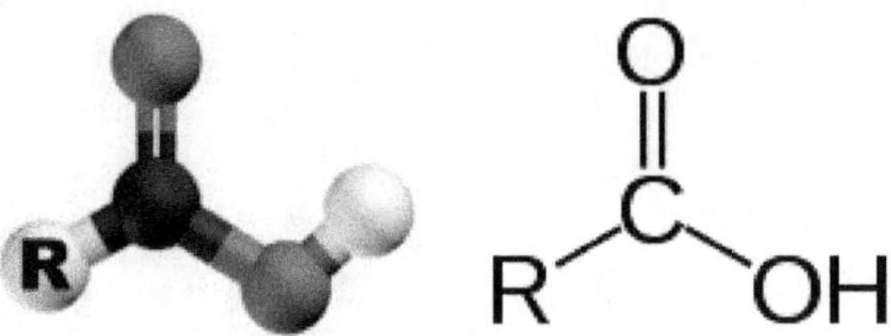

**CooH:** Nice … I see my C for carbon, double-O for oxygen, and hydrogen. I like the R. That's where I attach to things. Like your coffee. It has lots of acids in it – all with COOHs attached.

Or vinegar – it would just be water without me.

Some acids, like *malic acid*, have more than one COOH. It forms when fruit – like that banana over there – begins to turn brown and breakdown. I call it a COOH-sandwich.

**Publius:** That's interesting … I wanted to meet with you to learn more about fat and THC-COOH. I thought you might know why the body would store THC-COOH, the leftover-metabolite from cannabis use, in our fat.

**CooH:** Well, that seems obvious. It would be for later use. If you want a word, try ***"utility."***

**Publius:** Say more.

**CooH:** Life works by utility. Along the way, life made certain mammalian decisions and not others. Those decisions make your genetic code and point toward goals – like storing energy in fat for future use.

Fat as ***utility*** is the best answer; it's a declaration that life wants to live.

**Publius:** So you're saying THC-COOH in fat must be good otherwise our bodies are dumb and that genetics didn't know what it was doing.

**CooH:** Right.

**Publius:** Interesting … yet prohibition ruins lives because of you …

**CooH:** Yup. Your drug-testing culture does that, not me. In culture, I'm a ***misunderstood metabolite*** – not to your body though – it knows exactly what to do with me.

**Publius:** But the prohibitionists – they make it real. Real like you lose a job or don't get one. Real like calling the Department of Children's Services, revoking parole, taking licenses, and seizing assets. It's like you're the chemical fall guy.

**CooH:** I know … *people don't even ask what I'm doing in fat.*

**Publius:** Right! What is it you do?

**CooH:** I'm stable.

**Publius:** Okay …?

**CooH:** Well, this plant you love so much, it also stores THC as THC-COOH. Basically, as an acidic marker, I make THC storable.

**Publius:** In the plant and in us …

**CooH:** Right.

**Publius:** … in our fat.

**CooH:** Right again. When you heat cannabis, by fire or on a stove, the acidic marker (me) is ***decarboxylated***. That means I get released, unattached, from the THC.

Note that the other cannabinoids go through the same deal and become available to activate receptor systems.

After receptor activation, the liver begins to process cannabinoid metabolites from the body. During this activity I get reattached to THC for … oh, we'll say distribution.

**Publius:** Sometimes in famous pee …

**CooH:** Right – pee, poop, sweat, fat – stuff like that.
Yeah – famous pee moments. POTUS 40 Reagan and his VPOTUS 40 Bush – that was some mighty political pee for sure.

**Publius:** – Funny.

**CooH:** Hey – you asked. There's a whole laundry list of famous people getting caught up with the COOH. Lots of athletes: even Olympians.
Some folks lived in a time when they couldn't police me in humans – people like Mr. Armstrong and Mr. Dylan. In those days they didn't make'em pee in a cup. People had to get caught with the green-stuff back then – which is THC-COOH.
Ah, the early days of the cannabinoid war –

**Publius:** Nostalgic?

**CooH:** Yeah, I've had some good times, though it ain't cool to be caught-up by the COOH. It gives me a bad image.

**Publius:** The distribution to fat – *adipose tissue* – that's the one I want to talk about. It seems we are biologically programmed to store THC-COOH in fat.

**CooH:** Yes you are. It's genetic.

**Publius:** What happens though?

**CooH:** What do you mean? You have receptors genetically programmed into your mammalian genes …

**Publius:** Whatever, that's cool and all … it's just that there is this other reality, a political one, where THC-COOH in fat causes trouble for people. It's like you're an informant working for the other side, working against me and my friends …

**CooH:** You don't think I'm on your side? How can fat, as stored energy and not a norm of culture, be bad?

**Publius:** I don't know?

**CooH:** Well here's a fat fact: ***fat cells produce endocannabinoids***. Makes it easy to see why fat might be interested in THC-COOH. Fat can metabolize endocannabinoids, which also means it can metabolize herbal and pharmaceutical cannabinoids.

**Publius:** Right. That's why the cannabinoiders at Cayman Chemical don't think you're bad. They have this one chart online called *Arachidonic Acid Cascade* – which is Omega-6. You're all over that chart.

**CooH:** Yup – wherever there's acid, I'm there.
Funny how ideology works: citizens know more about dirty urine than they do about cannabinoids. You could call it an *outlier ideology* because it posits the outlier as the norm.

**Publius:** *Outlier ideology* … sounds like something prohibition would do.

**CooH:** THC-COOH is way more normal than people ever imagined.

**Publius:** I hear ya CooH.
Well, what if we call that a rap for today …

**CooH:** Sounds good – later P!

**Publius:** Later CooH! And stay in touch …

*Publius*
(2011)

### Search terms
Carboxylic acid; THC-COOH; adipose tissue (fat) and cannabinoids; Cayman Chemical's *CB1 Receptor Gene Map* and *Arachidonic Acid Cascade*; POTUS 40 and VPOTUS 40 peeing; Arno Hazekamp.

### Research and selected readings
2010: J Rohrich, et al, *Concentrations of delta9-tetrahydrocannabinol & 11-nor-9-carboxytetrahydrocannabinol in blood and urine after passive exposure to Cannabis smoke in a coffee shop*, Analytical Toxicology, 2010:34(4):196-203.

2008: C Pagano, et al, *Endocannabinoids, adipose tissue, and lipid metabolism*, Neuroendocrinology, May 2008:20 (Suppl 1):124-9.

2007: A Hazekamp, *Cannabis: extracting the medicine*, PrintPartners Ipskamp BV, Netherlands.

2006: B Spoto, et al, *Human adipose tissue binds and metabolizes the endocannabinoids anandamide and 2-arachidonoylglycerol*, Biochimie, December 2006:88(12):1889-97.

2004: S Young, *Ronald Reagan on drugs*, Drug Sense Weekly and November Coalition, 11 June 2004.

1996: D Baum, *Smoke and mirrors: the war on drugs and the politics of failure*, Little, Brown and Company, New York NY.

1984: J Johnson, et al, *Stability of delta 9-tetrahydrocannabinol (THC), 11-hydroxy-THC, and 11-nor-9-carboxy-THC in blood and plasma*, Analytical Toxicology, Sep-Oct 1984:8(5):202-4.

# #19

# Peeing to pay the mortgage

*U R in discrimination-land*

Jack Herer, an early hemp-champion, poked fun at our American sense of freedom by noting – *"Land of the free?"* More like *"Land of the pee."*

The Emperor of Hemp's words were ringing in my ears this day – and so was another word, "urine." Such a simple word, and it really has its place – in a toilet. So why was I peeing in a cup and not the toilet? There I was cup in hand and peeing-like a woman – because I am one. I'm also a professional and an independent contractor with years of consulting experience. However, this was the first time I ever had to pee like this – with a pass / fail attached to it.

Yes – I was required to surrender my pee in order to get a corporate contract.

I had that ***"Really?!"*** moment. It's called disbelief. I have decades of experience as both an independent contractor and working for a corporation. Six weeks earlier, I had completed a consulting contract with this same company. Now they needed my pee in order to pay me, as my urine was now mandated for employment. ***I submitted my pee in order to pay the mortgage***.

I also had this thought – taking my piss from me was too much, as if work doesn't take enough. An invasion of privacy is also too kind. They take something from you by making a demand. That's not an invasion of privacy. **Discrimination comes to mind – so does robbery.** You might be familiar with being robbed – I've been there and know how it feels. The robber says "Give me your money and don't make me hurt you." The boss says "Give me your pee and don't make me hurt you." *Not much difference* – in fact, that might be how to describe discrimination – *when you are asked to give up something, things like respect and dignity, in a moment of inequity.*

I peed out of economic necessity, though not without wondering what my pee had to do with the quality of my work. Since peeing I've learned that corporations often introduce the practice of testing in sly ways. They say things like "We are tightening up our process for hiring consultants" or "This is now part of our hiring process." This company also contracted a third-party vendor to implement the new policy. This eliminated the non-compliers – no pee, no job. This is called discrimination by weeding out.

I had the traditional pee-test. I went to the white-coats and used their plastic cup in their certified lab. And in a moment of synchronicity, I submitted what they referred to as "specimen" to the white-coat at the perfect time of 4:20.

Interesting my use of the word "submitted." It felt like submission. If I didn't submit my specimen – there would be no job and no way to pay the mortgage. If I didn't pee and pass, I wouldn't get the work. I left my pee, was thanked by the white-coat, and then had to wait about a week to hear if I passed. I had studied for the test (it's also called abstaining), so passing was likely.

The laboratory is paid to run tests on your specimen. The consulting firm that contracted the white-coats receives only a simple "Positive" (with a list of substances in violation) or "Negative" with no further information.

Wait a second – I gave you my urine so that you could analyze it for what? *I wanted to know what was in my pee.*

I phoned the pee-testing center and asked what drugs they tested for? They said this information could not be given to me because I did not pay for the pee-screen. I then asked the consulting firm to please provide me with a copy of the pee-report. After much delay by human-resource-coats, I was finally given the report on my urine. It said I passed. I wasn't surprised, like I said, I had studied – it was just anticlimactic and not what I wanted to know. They took a personal part of me and gave me back a message of "Negative" and called it good.

That's weird. I feel like they pissed-on one of my rights. Submitting my urine for a job opportunity in which a content analysis of my lifestyle is for THC-COOH, seems beyond strange to me. What happened to that once cherished right? The one a famed and progressive US Supreme Court Justice said was ***the most comprehensive of rights and the right most valued by civilized men.***

Martin Luther King, Jr. had a dream, and so do I. I dream about adults one day living in a nation where they aren't judged by the THC-COOH in their urine, but by the content of their character. Like King's dream, mine too would make a better nation.

The focus of work is quality – not the levels of a metabolite. Depressants like alcohol, antidepressants like Prozac, and stimulants like sugar are commonly practiced and accepted in our workforce, as the "drug-free" workplace is a myth of prohibition. There is also no scientific evidence supporting the idea that THC-COOH is detrimental or causes harm on the job – in fact, a workplace *is* about activating your ECS. No one can work without an ECS, so it makes little sense to police the levels of an inactive metabolite. – Unless you happen to be a prohibitionist.

I also learned this fact about THC-COOH policing: if you are taking a prescription for Marinol, a synthetic cannabinoid that also leaves the metabolite THC-COOH in your urine, you get a pharmaceutical pass. Yes, in drug war logic, one kind of THC-COOH, the one from the plant, is "Positively Bad" and the THC-COOH from the pharmaceutical company is "Positively Okay." I'm pretty sure that's called hypocrisy.

Speaking of hypocrisy, it is difficult to defend pee-tests on the grounds of public safety. If that was a valid argument, then police and fire personnel across America would face the tests. But most don't. And, pee-tests would check for alcohol – but that's a different story.

In the end, who benefits? Drug testing companies seem to be the biggest winner – to the tune of millions. As for the workers, the companies, and basic liberty in America, it's a losing proposition.

*'Land of the free and home of the brave'* – just like Jack Herer, Martin Luther King, Jr. and that Supreme Court Justice who saw privacy as a fundamental right – that's where I want to live.

*Publius*
*(2011)*

### Search terms
Health and cannabinoids; drug testing industry; Hayek and coercion; Justice Brandeis and the right to be let alone; Jack Herer (1939-2010).

### Research and selected readings
2010: M Catani, et al, *Human platelets express authentic CB1 and CB2 receptors*, Current Neurovascular Research, November 2010:7(4):311-8.

2010: C Quarta, et al, *CB1 signaling in forebrain and sympathetic neurons is a key determinant of endocannabinoid actions on energy balance*, Cell Metabolism, April 2010:11(4):273-85.

2010: C Ziegler, et al, *Expression and function of endocannabinoid receptors in the human adrenal cortex*, Hormone and Metabolic Research, February 2010:42(2):88-92.

2009: G Reisfield, et al, *'False-positive' and 'false negative' test results in clinical urine drug testing*, Bioanalysis, August 2009:1(5):937-52.

2008: G Beato, *Golden Age – How Americans learned to stop worrying and love workplace drug testing*, Reason, March 2008.

2006: S Levy, et al, *Drug testing in adolescents in ambulatory medicine: physician practices and knowledge*, Archives of Pediatrics & Adolescent Medicine, February 2006:160(2):146-50.

2002: M Gray, ed., *Busted: stone cowboys, narco-lords, and Washington's war on drugs*, Thunder's Mouth Press, New York NY.

1991: D Harvey, et al, *Urinary metabolites of cannabidiol in dog, rat and man and their identification by gas chromatography mass spectrometry*, Chromatography, January 1991:562(1-2):299-322.

1980: J Cunha, et al, *Chronic administration of cannabidiol to healthy volunteers and epileptic patients*, Pharmacology, 1980:21(3):175-85.

1960: F Hayek, *The constitution of liberty*, University of Chicago Press, Chicago IL.

_______________     _______________________

*[Cannabis], in its natural form, is one of the safest therapeutically active substances known . . . It would be unreasonable, arbitrary, and capricious for the DEA to continue to stand between those sufferers and the benefits of this substance.*

> Francis L. Young
> DEA Chief Administrative Law Judge
> 1988

_______________          _______________________

#20

# Patently wrong *(since 2003)*

*Knowledge is power.*

Francis Bacon

I know more about cannabinoids than anyone in the DEA. I know more about cannabis than many professional scientists. These are topics I've been inspired to research for years.

I work as an independent writer and researcher. While I am sometimes hired by others to research and write about the subjects that interest them, cannabis is a subject that interests me.

What I know from that research is that thousands of scientists around the world understand the value of cannabinoids. Cannabis users understand that same value, however for decades we've been baffled about how to make the US government understand what we understand.

Since cannabis is defined as a Schedule I drug by the Controlled Substances Act, it appears that our federal government believes cannabis has "no medical value" – the primary standard for a substance to be placed on Schedule I. Simultaneously, it is also a federal crime to possess any amount of cannabis.

How, I've puzzled, can I get the right facts before the federal government? As it turns out, the feds already know. Our government, and therefore *We the People*, already understand the value of cannabinoids because *We own a patent on them*.

Whoa! – Stop right there – that can't be right, can it? After the billions of dollars spent to stop cannabis, after the millions arrested merely for possessing cannabis, the federal government took the trouble to patent cannabis?

Don't take my word for it – go look it up. The patent number is 6,630,507. This is not the paranoid fantasy of an independent researcher. It's there in black and white, part of the federal record, for the whole world to see. To quote:

> *"The cannabinoids are found to have particular application as neuroprotectants, for example in limiting neurological damage following ischemic insults, such as stroke and trauma, or in the treatment of neurodegenerative diseases, such as Alzheimer's disease, Parkinson's disease and HIV dementia."*

So, one federal agency recognizes cannabinoids as the miracle that they are (the US Patent Office), while another federal agency will do anything to prevent people from researching them in their natural whole form (the DEA).

On the surface, this is illogical. If cannabinoids are good enough to patent, surely they are good enough to allow medical research. But you may be thinking of conventional logic that dictates decisions based on the best outcome for the most people. There is another kind of logic – the logic of authoritarian control and repression. If nothing else, the federal government's contradictory position on cannabinoids shows that one thing is understood by those in authority: this is a mighty powerful plant.

Again, this is clear in the patent:

> ## US Patent #6,630,507
>
> Cannabinoids have been found to have antioxidant properties, unrelated to NMDA receptor antagonism. This new found property makes cannabinoids useful in the treatment and prophylaxis of wide variety of oxidation associated diseases, such as ischemic, age-related, inflammatory and autoimmune diseases. ***The cannabinoids are found to have particular application as neuroprotectants, for example in limiting neurological damage following ischemic insults, such as stroke and trauma, or in the treatment of neurodegenerative diseases, such as Alzheimer's disease, Parkinson's disease and HIV dementia.*** Nonpsychoactive cannabinoids, such as cannabidoil [sic], are particularly advantageous to use because they avoid toxicity that is encountered with psychoactive cannabinoids at high doses useful in the method of the present invention. A particular disclosed class of cannabinoids useful as neuroprotective antioxidants is formula (I) wherein the R group is independently selected from the group consisting of H, CH.sub.3, and COCH.sub.3.

This is *Our* patent, one owned by *We the People* since 2003. Today there is an **additional eight years** of scientific research showing cannabinoid benefits that weren't even imagined back when the patent was granted. The People own the patent: the DEA does not own the People.

As the scientists continue to confirm, particularly in light of a contradictory and hostile government, we would all be wise to continue our independent research projects – not only in libraries and the Internet, but out in the field as well. The scientists will back us up, even if our government won't.

Authoritarian forces within the government will try to maintain their stranglehold on cannabinoids, but those authoritarian forces will fail eventually. Cannabinoids are just too powerful – and *We* own the patent.

Look it up!

*Publius*
(2011)

## Search terms
US Patent 6,630,507; US Patent 2,304,669; cannabinoids and oxidation associated diseases; Alzheimer's, Parkinson's, and HIV dementia; Schedule I CSA; *Health Professionals for Responsible Drug Scheduling.*

## Research and selected readings
2011: K Kamprath, et al, *Short-term adaptation of conditioned fear responses through endocannabinoid signaling in the central amygdala*, American College of Neuropsychopharmacology, February 2011:36(3):652-63.

2011: V Pisani, et al, *Homeostatic changes of the endocannabinoid system in Parkinson's disease*, Movement Disorders, February 2011:26(2):216-22.

2010: M Rajesh, et al, *Cannabidiol attenuates cardiac dysfunction, oxidative stress, fibrosis, and inflammatory and cell death signaling pathways in diabetic cardiomyopathy*, American College of Cardiology, December 2010:56(25):2115-25.

2010: J Marcu, et al, *Cannabidiol enhances the inhibitory effects of delta9-tetrahydrocannabinol on human glioblastoma cell proliferation and survival*, Molecular Cancer Therapeutics, January 2010:9(1):180-9.

2009: M Galal, et al, *Naturally occurring and related synthetic cannabinoids and their potential therapeutic applications*, Recent Patents on CNS Drug Discovery, June 2009:4(2):112-36.

2008: R Pertwee, *The diverse CB1 and CB2 receptor pharmacology of three plant cannabinoids: delta9-tetrahydrocannabinol, cannabidiol, and delta9-tetrahydrocannabivarin*, British Journal of Pharmacology, January 2008:153(2):199-215.

2006: R McKallip, et al, *Cannabidiol-induced apoptosis in human leukemia cells: a novel role for cannabidiol in the regulation of p22phox and Nox4 expression*, Molecular Pharmacology, September 2006:70(3):897-908.

2004: M Diana and A Marty, *Endocannabinoid-mediated short-term synaptic plasticity: depolarization-induced suppression of inhibition (DSI) and depolarization-induced suppression of excitation (DSE)*, British Journal of Pharmacology, May 2004:142(1):9-19.

2002: P Zygmunt, *Delta 9-tetrahydrocannabinol and cannabinol activate capsaicin-sensitive sensory nerves via a CB1 and CB2 cannabinoid receptor-independent mechanism*, Neuroscience, June 2002:22(11):4720-7.

2001: T Maejima, et al, *Endogenous cannabinoid as a retrograde messenger from depolarized postsynaptic neurons to presynaptic terminals*, Neuroscience Research, July 2001:40(3):205-10.

1996: D Abrams and MPP, *Medical marijuana – once again – blocked*, Critical Path AIDS Project, Fall 1996:(No 31):21.

1994: D Abrams, *Donald Abrams' marijuana study*, Critical Path AIDS Project, Winter 1994-95:(No 30):9-17.

1942: R Adams, US Patent 2,304,669, *Isolation of Cannabidiol*, Urbana IL, 8 December 1942.

#21


*"Hi, my name is Publius and I have been an alcoholic since 1972."*


These words are unfortunately familiar to many. Such words uttered daily in thousands of Alcoholic Anonymous (AA) facilities did not work for me. I would go to AA meetings with an open but often still–inebriated mind. The stories were the problem. Those awful, all-too-human stories told by people about alcohol and its destructive ways. The tales of devastation would leave me so distressed / distraught that I would want to leave and go get a drink. I felt no solace or sympathy at these meetings – just loneliness and despair.

My alcoholism continued on its not so merry way until my doctor began to convince me of something I would come to know: that drinking alcohol and living long were not compatible. I quit drinking one day in the 1990s, exactly when does not matter, although truly I don't recall. Even though I had rejected AA as a source of assistance, I was not without help. I had health insurance and an encouraging doctor. He endorsed the use of cannabis to offset the symptoms of alcohol withdrawal – the harshest symptom being death. He also recommended a psychiatrist. With their help, along with family and friends, I stopped using and abusing alcohol.

I call the period from 1973 to 1983 my dark-drunk decade. I know it is eleven years – like I said, it was dark. Life became a never-ending dimly-lit tunnel. Sure, there was a light at the end of the tunnel – but I never reached or got any closer to it.

You could also say I lost my light chasing an alcohol "high." I want to make a distinction between the high one gets from alcohol and the high produced by cannabinoids and the ECS. Knowing your high is important – like how an alcohol high will make you low. A cannabinoid high doesn't work that way. No one suggests people who are high on anandamide should be arrested for driving after a run in the park. Yet they are high – i.e., the runner's high from the endocannabinoid anandamide and the ECS. And no one should be arrested for the ***"elevated sense of well-being"*** mentioned on the warning label of the pharmaceutical cannabinoid Marinol.

How did cannabis help after I quit drinking alcohol? For me, it worked like a crutch. I had tried to quit alcohol many times. I was never successful until I used cannabis. Little did I know I was supplementing my ECS. A quick search of PubMed reveals how cannabinoids help. One report from 2007 is even titled ***"The endocannabinoid signaling system: a potential target for next-generation therapeutics for alcoholism."*** Looks like me and lots of researchers agree – cannabinoids help overcome alcoholism.

Was it necessary? Seems so – and it worked. I'm no longer a drunk. You can call me a pothead, yeah, or even a cannabinoider. But you can't call me a drunk. Like I mentioned, I quit with the help of doctors, family and friends, and what I call a cannabis crutch. The last time I quit drinking I was pretty determined that I was going to be successful. And I was. I don't know if I could have quit without cannabis supplementing my ECS: what I do know is that cannabis made the alcohol withdrawal easier.

Cannabis can also curb the amount of alcohol consumption by being an alternative for relaxation. Many people conclude their workday with a beer or glass of wine. If cannabis were a legal alternative, some people would choose it instead of alcohol. It would be hard to call that a bad thing – especially given the research surrounding the ECS.

Alcohol prohibition failed and we now have a regulated and taxed market for alcohol production, distribution and consumption.

The problems caused by alcohol are not going to be solved by outlawing its responsible use.

In a regulated and taxed market for adult cannabinoid use, different herbal cannabinoids (strains) would be regulated and tested to ensure consistent potency levels. Testing is already happening in medical states. Patients and dispensaries are using scientific techniques to determine which cannabinoids help different conditions – hence trusted products.

There would still be problems with a regulated and taxed market, such as zoning and civil liberties, but not the problems of prohibition. Such issues can be dealt with at the local level – where most of the taxes should stay.

Also, people who enjoy cannabis are similar to those who enjoy quality cigars, fine wines or organic foods. These groups share a discriminating taste for high quality items and are willing to pay more. They are selective and can interpret distinctions from one product to the next. *Cannabis connoisseurs* do the same thing. They will tell you in great detail the difference between strains just like one would describe the bouquets from different wines. For some it's a hobby and to others a serious business.

Either way, the violence associated with the cannabis market is violence caused by the state. By keeping cannabis in the illicit market, the state becomes complicit in the negative effects of its law. Until we end this prohibition, cannabis will be subject to the same practices that made Al Capone a household name.

*Publius*
*(2010)*


### Search terms

Alcoholism; alcohol withdrawal syndrome; alcohol prohibition; PubMed ethanol cannabinoids; International Association for Cannabinoid Medicines (IACM); Safer Alternative for Enjoyable Recreation (SAFER).

**Research and selected readings**


2010: A El-Remessy, et al, *Cannabidiol protects retinal neurons by preserving glutamine synthetase activity in diabetes*, Molecular Vision, August 2010:16:1487-95.

2010: M Roberto, et al, *The endocannabinoid system tonically regulates inhibitory transmission and depresses the effect of ethanol in central amygdala*, Neuropsychopharmacology, August 2010:35(9):1962-72.

2010: V Purohit, et al, *Role of cannabinoids in the development of fatty liver (steatosis)*, AAPS, June 2010:12(2):233-7.

2007: E Onaivi, *An endocannabinoid hypothesis of drug reward,* IACM – Cannabinoids, 2007:2(3):22-6.

2007: B Basavarajappa, *The endocannabinoid signaling system: a potential target for next-generation therapeutics for alcoholism,* Mini Reviews in Medicinal Chemistry, August 2007:7(8):769-79.

2006: K Vinod, et al, *Effect of chronic ethanol exposure and its withdrawal on the endocannabinoid system*, Neurochemistry International, November 2006:49(6):619-25.

2005: K Vinod and B Hungund, *Endocannabinoid lipids and mediated system: implications for alcoholism and neuropsychiatric disorders*, Life Sciences, August 2005:77(14):1569-83.

2002: B Basavarajappa and B Hungund, *Neuromodulatory role of the endocannabinoid signaling system in alcoholism: an overview*, Prostaglandins, Leukotrienes, and Essential Fatty Acids, February-March 2002:66(2-3):287-99.

1984: A Dvilansky, et al, *Effects of ethanol, CBD and delta 'THC on proliferation of K-562 cells*, International Journal of Tissue Reactions, 1984:6(5):409-12.

1979: B Belgrave, et al, *The effect of cannabidiol, alone and in combination with ethanol, on human performance,* Psychopharmacology (Berl), August 1979:64(2):243-6.

1970: T Mikuriya, *Cannabis substitution: an adjunctive therapeutic tool in the treatment of alcoholism,* Medical Times, April 1970:98(4):187-91.

#22

# 2-AG protects spinal cord injury

*Moreover, in the preserved white matter, 2-AG protects myelin from damage and reduces oligodendrocyte loss.*

In writing these essays, we had to learn how to read PubMed. We laughed a lot trying to pronounce the unfamiliar science. We gleaned here and there. We kept meeting, asking, writing and learning. Like all newbies, we were overwhelmed by the amount of information. Soon we started to notice various patterns. One was the investigation into activating and blocking cannabinoid activity. It is referred to as "agonist" for activating and "antagonist" for blocking receptors.

It was also clear that there was great interest in understanding cannabinoids – at the research level. **PubMed is a free database of references and abstracts on life sciences and biomedical topics maintained by the US National Library of Medicine at the National Institutes of Health.** It's a place where fact *beats* fiction. To the thousands of white-coats publishing in the journals posted on PubMed, cannabinoids are fascinatingly intriguing. We knew we could rely on their expertise – ***if we could only decipher it***.

Here's a technique we found useful. We would begin by deconstructing the abstract and interpreting each sentence. This allows one to see the theories, evidence and conclusions in their own framework. For example, the one we're going to breakdown in this essay is about the ***endocannabinoid 2-arachidonoyl glycerol***. The problem with the name is obvious, as it is with most cannabinoids, so everyone calls this one *2-AG*.

A PubMed search of this endocannabinoid returns nearly a thousand publications. We chose one from 2010 and published in Neurobiology of Disease. The title first caught our attention:

*The endocannabinoid 2-arachidonoyl glycerol reduces lesion expansion and white matter damage after spinal cord injury*

That's a long title to make a clear point: ***2-AG reduces the damage after spinal cord injury***.

Now let's read the abstract to see what support they have to test such a fantastic theory as the ECS reducing the damage of spinal cord injury. How can this be?

*1)  A series of pathological events secondary to spinal cord injury (SCI) contribute to the spread of the damage, which aggravates neurological deficits.*

Sounds like beyond the initial damage from the injury, there are a series of events that also cause harm:

*2)  Here we report that a single dose of the neuroprotective endocannabinoid 2-arachidonoyl glycerol (2-AG) administered early after SCI reduces lesion expansion, which was prevented by simultaneous blockade of both CB1 and CB2 receptors but not by blockade of either receptor alone.*

Okay. The white-coats dosed a rodent (mouse or rat most likely) with 2-AG right after SCI. This reduced the "lesion expansion" – the harm. They know this because they blocked CB1 and CB2 receptors and stopped this from happening. They also found that they had to block them both:

*3)   Treatment with 2-AG also preserves the white matter around the epicenter of the injury.*

Well, the preservation of "white matter" sounds important. A check of spinal cord on Wikipedia tells us that "Columns of white matter carry information either up or down the spinal cord." Yes, that's important:

*4)   Moreover, in the preserved white matter, 2-AG protects myelin from damage and reduces oligodendrocyte loss.*

**Bingo!** That's the sentence that makes this one so important. Oligodendrocytes build myelin. This is bordering on amazing ...

*5)   In addition to these protective actions at the epicenter region, 2-AG also inhibits the myelin damage and delayed oligodendrocyte loss induced at 10mm from the epicenter.*

Yes, there's amazing! Not only is 2-AG protective at the place of injury, it also inhibits myelin damage and delayed oligodendrocyte loss. That means the "myelinators" will be around to remyelin the damage:

*6)   Interestingly, the early protective action of 2-AG is maintained 28 days after injury, when the lesion size is still smaller and the preservation of white matter is better in 2-AG-treated animals.*

Yes, *interestingly*. After a month the injuries treated with the cannabinoid were better off. Interesting indeed:

*7)   Therefore, our results show that 2-AG protects from the expansion of the lesion and white matter damage, which suggest that this endogenous cannabinoid may be useful as a protective treatment for acute SCI.*

The white-coats report that the *endo 2-AG protects from the damage caused by acute spinal cord injury*.

There, that wasn't so difficult.

Cannabis as a means to cannabinoid supplementation should be noted for its properties – not its politics. The PubMed world knows this. As we learn more and more about cannabinoids and the ECS, the harm we are causing is becoming clear. Prohibition isn't just about taking our liberty; it also takes away possibilities – *like protecting our spinal cords*.

*Publius*
(2011)


**Search terms**
PubMed, 2-AG and diacylglycerol lipase; oligodendrocytes; cannabinoids and SCI/neuroprotection; remyelination.


**Research and selected readings**
2011: L Zhang, et al, *Endocannabinoids generated by Ca2+ or by metabotropic glutamate receptors appear to arise from different pools of diacylglycerol lipase*, PLoS One, January 2011:6(1):e16305.

2010: A Arevalo-Martin, et al, *The endocannabinoid 2-arachidonoyl glycerol reduces lesion expansion and white matter damage after spinal cord injury*, Neurobiology of Disease, May 2010:38(2):304-12.

2010: C Fichtner, *Cannabinomics: the marijuana policy tipping point*, Well Mind Books, Chicago IL.

2009: P Nagarkatti, et al, *Cannabinoids as novel anti-inflammatory drugs*, Future Medicinal Chemistry, October 2009:1(7):1333-49.

2009: S Mato, et al, *CB1 cannabinoid receptor-dependent and - independent inhibition of depolarization-induced calcium influx in oligodendrocytes*, Glia, February 2009:57(3):295-306.

2008: A Arevalo-Martin, et al, *CB2 cannabinoid receptors as an emerging target for demyelinating diseases: from neuroimmune interactions to cell replacement strategies*, British Journal of Pharmacology, January 2008:153(2):216-25.

2007: J Blackman, et al, *A comprehensive profile of brain enzymes that hydrolyze the endocannabinoid 2-arachidonoylglycerol*, Chemistry & Biology, December 2007:14(12):1347-56.

2007: F Docagne, et al, *Excitotoxicity in a chronic model of multiple sclerosis: neuroprotective effects of cannabinoids through CB1 and CB2 receptor activation*, Molecular and Cellular Neurosciences, April 2007:34(4):551-61.

2005: T Maejima, et al, *Synaptically driven endocannabinoid release requires Ca2+-assisted metabotropic glutamate receptor subtype 1 to phospholipase Cbeta4 signaling cascade in the cerebellum*, Neuroscience, July 2005:25(29):6826-35.

2001: R Mechoulam and L Hanu, *The cannabinoids: an overview. Therapeutic implications in vomiting and nausea after cancer chemotherapy, in appetite promotion, in multiple sclerosis and in neuroprotection*, Pain Research & Management, Summer 2001:6(2):67-73.

#23

# Think of the children: prohibition creates crime …
## *and obesity*

> *The prestige of government has undoubtedly been lowered considerably by the prohibition law. For nothing is more destructive of respect for the government and the law of the land than passing laws which cannot be enforced. It is an open secret that the dangerous increase of crime in this country is closely connected with this.*

Albert Einstein, *The World As I See It (1931)*

Three teens are detained by two police. The officers are in civilian clothes and drive an unmarked squad car. Two of the three teens are dressed in high school uniforms – white t-shirt and black pants. The teens assume the *"put your hands on the trunk"* position. One officer searches their pockets, routinely emptying the contents onto the trunk of the squad car. At one point the searching officer shows one of the teens a green item in a plastic baggie. Suddenly the world became black and white.

*Think of the children?*

We do. We'll think of them as they are welcomed into state detention centers and jails for baggie-size cannabis violations. We'll think of them as they and their families cope with a new reality.

Now they are part of the 800,000 cannabis arrests feeding America's drug war diet. That diet is ravenous and pernicious. Prohibition doesn't think of the children – that's why we have to.

In doing so we found a new theory: **what if prohibition creates obesity?**

This theory sounds odd at first, sort of like our earlier moment of *"You want pregnant women to ~~smoke~~ consume pot?"* This new moment would be – *"You want children to ~~smoke~~ consume pot?"*

Let's go all **Albert** for a minute. We can **Einstein** this theory on PubMed by beginning with the failure of Rimonabant, a synthetic cannabinoid intended to be the answer for America's obesity problem. This synthetic cannabinoid was designed to block the CB1 receptor. They thought this would stop you from being hungry – **from getting the munchies**. It didn't work. Why? Stopping obesity is more than just turning the CB1 receptor off. To modulate diet, you have to simultaneously turn on parts of the ECS while blocking others.

So the pharmaceuticals started with the idea that if you smoke pot you will get the munchies and it will make you fat. The idea that cannabinoids are involved in energy intake (munchies) is a given. So if cannabinoids are a potential obesity-buster, there would be research on **activating and not just blocking cannabinoid receptors** – research like this:

> 2011: *While initially it was believed that this* **endocannabinoid signaling system** *would only facilitate energy intake, we now know that perhaps even more important functions of endocannabinoids and CB(1) receptors in this context are to* **enhance energy storage into the adipose tissue and reduce energy expenditure by influencing both lipid and glucose metabolism.**

So the ECS functions to enhance energy storage and reduce energy expenditure. That's called homeostasis, or how a system maintains balance. Let's click again:

> 2010: ***Cannabinoids*** *have been shown to* ***act as potent immunosuppressive and anti-inflammatory*** *agents and have been shown to mediate beneficial effects in a wide* ***range of immune-mediated*** *diseases such as multiple sclerosis,* ***diabetes****, septic shock, rheumatoid arthritis, and allergic asthma.*

Here we have a connection to diabetes and other immune-mediated diseases. We also know that obesity is characterized by chronic inflammation. Systems such as adipose tissue (fat) become overstressed:

> 2010: ***The endocannabinoids, anandamide and 2-AG, are produced by adipocytes****, where they stimulate lipogenesis via cannabinoid CB1 receptors and are under the negative control of leptin and insulin.*
>
> ***The observed alterations emphasize, for the first time in humans, the potential different role and regulation of adipose tissue anandamide (and its congeners) and 2-AG in obesity and type 2 diabetes.***

This is the point where ***"Prohibition creates obesity"*** moves from the theoretical to the practiced. American youth are bombarded with anti-drug messages that equate "marijuana" with a methamphetamine-like menace. Two out of three American homes have a regular user of drugs – prescription drugs that is. That's a lot of access for our children to these lethal-yet-legal drugs. Cannabinoids are not lethal. This mixed-messaging has to confuse the young.

It's time to begin ***the cannabinoid education campaign***. This part of health class has to be de-propagandized. The health of our children depends on it. We are at risk from our government's campaign against "marijuana," as obesity and type 2 diabetes are not theoretical; they are threats.

We think Einstein would agree: *"For nothing is more destructive of respect for the government and the law of the land than passing laws which cannot be enforced."*

*Publius*
(2011)

## Search terms

Adipose tissue, adipocytes, lipogenesis and cannabinoids; oleic acid; Albert Einstein; Unconventional Foundation for Autism (UF4A); Rimonabant; Ben Harper's *People Lead.*

## Research and selected readings

2011: V Di Marzo, et al, *Cannabinoids and endocannabinoids in metabolic disorders with focus on diabetes*, Handbook of Experimental Pharmacology, 2011:(203):75-104.

2011: M Li and B Cheung, *Rise and fall of anti-obesity drugs*, World Journal of Diabetes, February 2011:2(2):19-23.

2010: O Mahmood, et al, *Learning and memory performances in adolescent users of alcohol and marijuana: interactive effects*, Studies on Alcohol and Drugs, November 2010:71(6):885-94.

2010: S Rieder, et al, *Cannabinoid-induced apoptosis in immune cells as a pathway to immunosuppression*, Immunobiology, August 2010:215(8):598-605.

2010: G Annuzzi, et al, *Differential alterations of the concentrations of endocannabinoids and related lipids in the subcutaneous adipose tissue of obese diabetic patients*, Lipids in Health and Disease, April 2010:9:43.

2010: J Sipe, et al, *Biomarkers of endocannabinoid system activation in severe obesity*, PLoS One, January 2010:5(1):e8792.

2008: D Cota, *Role of the endocannabinoid system in energy balance regulation and obesity*, Frontiers of Hormone Research, 2008:36:135-45.

2008: A Samat, et al, *Rimonabant [SR141716] for the treatment of obesity*, Recent Patents on Cardiovascular Drug Discovery, November 2008:3(3):187-93.

2007: C Pagano, et al, *The endogenous cannabinoid system stimulates glucose uptake in human fat cells via phosphatidylinositol 3-kinase and calcium-dependent mechanisms*, Clinical Endocrinology and Metabolism, December 2007:92(12):4810-9.

2006: P Trayhurn, et al, *Adipose tissue and adipokines – energy regulation from the human perspective*, Nutrition, July 2006:136(7 Suppl):1935S-9S.

2005: D Jeffries and L Jeffries, *Jeffrey's journey: healing a violent child's rage*, Quick American Archives, Oakland CA.

2005: S Engli, et al, *Activation of the peripheral endocannabinoid system in human obesity*, Diabetes, October 2005:54(10):2838-43.

2004: J Miron, *Drug war crimes: the consequences of prohibition*, Independent Institute, Oakland CA.

1931: A Einstein, *The world as I see it*, Forum and Century: 13th in the Living Philosophies series, 1931:84:193-4.

#24

# Pushing back in Montana

*Liberty in the 21<sup>st</sup> century*

I toured Montana in April 2007 to help patients and organizers unite to move their new state medical cannabis policy forward. Also on the tour were Angel Raich, the terminally ill patient who unsuccessfully sued the federal government over its harassment of California patients, and Debby Goldsberry, who founded Cannabis Action Network (CAN) and runs the Berkeley Patients Group, one of America's oldest and largest medical cannabis dispensaries.

At that time, Montana had a decent medical cannabis law on the books for over a year. The problem was widespread fear and confusion about how to safely grow and acquire medicine. For instance, we met many people whose legal number of plants produced more usable medicine than they were allowed; they were looking for legal ways to distribute their extra cannabinoids to patients in need. We also met nurses working in rural areas where doctors are rare, and they expressed the need for revisions to the law that would allow rural nurse practitioners and other medical staff to recommend herbal cannabinoids. Montana also has an extremely high percentage of war veterans, so many of the concerned patients were vets who felt they would never find a doctor or affordable medicine.

We found lots of good news. Montana has dedicated and talented organizers with local and national support for developing legal medical access for patients. For example, in a state of only one million, there were already over 100 doctors recommending cannabis! Our public audience was only around 20 at each event, but they were interested, articulate, and each group was comprised of a different 20 people.

We found by immersing ourselves in the local scene that we could best know how to advise patients and families. Montanans (and their economy) are quiet and move at a slower pace. Homogeneous culture is the norm. Most Montanans don't lock their house or car doors, lots of people carry handguns, and everyone we met was very relaxed and kind. Many areas were without cell phone and recycling services. People looking for organic or vegetarian food had a few options, such as *The Good Food Store* in Missoula or *The Community Co-op* in Bozeman.

The main theme of our journey through the state was "marijuana IS medicine." We also stuck to the ever-important philosophies of sensible use, knowing your rights during police encounters, and respecting the beautiful and liberating nature of cannabis. For instance, our first event was a "Schools Not Prisons" rally on the University of Montana campus in Missoula on 4-20. It was organized by the new chapter of Students for Sensible Drug Policy (SSDP), and included a DJ and several speakers. We set up the CAN booth and listened while the chapter's president read horrific statistics about the drug war. Angel and Debby spoke about medical cannabis and California, and called on students to get involved to help patients in Montana. The rally culminated in a "Know Your Rights" legal training workshop. The SSDP vice-president and I played cops and audience members were our citizen-victims. Debby narrated, and we taught everyone the magic words: *"I choose to remain silent and want to see my lawyer."*

Later that day, we rallied at the County Courthouse and marched the few blocks to the Federal Courthouse. There were many empowering speeches, drums, signs, and even a few joints passed around! Angel said, "Montana patients can learn a lot from

California. That is because we've really scraped our knees as we've implemented our law." Her words resonated with the Montana patients, who pledged to continue meeting and working to improve their law.

The rally was also the first time Robin Prosser, a well-known patient, met Angel. Robin had recently had her medicine taken by the DEA, but at this moment was not facing any charges.

In October 2007, Prosser committed suicide. I'm reminded of the priests who self-immolated by fire in Vietnam during that war. Maybe it's just another war, another death, and another … opportunity lost.

There is a concerted push-back against cannabis reform. It's not as if a law is passed and patients live happily ever after. The evidence is in California, Colorado, Oregon and other pioneering states. It's also in Montana and Michigan, where state and DEA task forces raid dispensaries. Montana voted 62% to allow medical cannabis. Michigan's medical law won in all 82 counties. These aren't hippy states, yet citizens like Robin Prosser die while the country waits – waits for what?

The citizens in medical cannabis states have spoken. Not everyone is listening.

*Publius*
*(2011)*

### Search terms
Angel Raich; Debby Goldsberry; Robin Prosser; Montana and Michigan medical cannabis programs; Veterans, PTSD and cannabinoids; Sections 11 & 15 of the Illinois Cannabis Control Act.

### Research and selected readings
2011: D Frosch, *Marijuana for Post-Traumatic Stress Disorder may be studied*, New York Times, 18 July.

2011: D Vara, et al, *Anti-tumoral action of cannabinoids on heptacellular carcinoma: role of AMPK-dependent activation of autophagy*, Cell Death and Differentiation, July 2011:18(7):1099-111.

2011: K Nithipatikom, et al, *Anti-proliferative effect of a putative endocannabinoid, 2-arachidonoyl glycerol ether in prostate carcinoma cells*, Prostaglandins & other Lipid Mediators, February 2011:94(1-2):34-43.

2010:  V Di Marzo, *Anandamide serves two masters in the brain*, Nature Neuroscience, December 2010:13(12):1446-8.

2010: D Frosch, *V.A. easing rules for users of medical marijuana*, New York Times, 23 July.

2010:  S Bhattacharyya, et al, *Opposite effects of delta-9-tetrahydrocannabinol and cannabidiol on human brain function and psychopathology*, Neuropsychopharmacology, February 2010:35(3):764-74.

2009: K Taber and R Hurley, *Endocannabinoids: stress, anxiety, and fear*, Neuropsychiatry and Clinical Neurosciences, Spring 2009:21(2): iv, 109-13.

2007: P Lafenetre, et al, *The endocannabinoid system in the processing of anxiety and fear and how CB1 receptors may modulate fear extinction*, Pharmacological Research, November 2007:56(5):367-81.

2000: B Hungund and B Basavarajappa, *Are anandamide and cannabinoid receptors involved in ethanol tolerance? A review of the evidence,* Alcohol and Alcoholism, Mar-Apr 2000:35(2):126-33.

1942: S Allentuck and K Bowman, *Psychiatric aspects of marihuana intoxication*, American Journal of Psychiatry, 1942:99:248-51.

# Part Three: and the Pursuit of Happiness

*Punishment for using a drug should not be more harmful to an individual than the drug itself.*

POTUS 39, Jimmy Carter
1978

#25

# Bliss ain't ignorant

*Most folks are about as happy as they make up their minds to be.*

POTUS 16 Lincoln

**The Bliss Copy** is considered the authentic version of Lincoln's Gettysburg Address because he signed it. Let's expand the metaphor for our last section – *The Bliss Copy* – when putting your name to an action signifies the truth.

The initial Publius stood up to a king and became known as the founder of the Roman Republic. He died in 503 BC. Centuries later a future Roman emperor named a son Publius. This second Publius, the one who died in 53 AD, shadows the first Publius in our work. The founders we honor, Alexander Hamilton, James Madison and John Jay, would have known the stories of both Romans: the first Publius as hero, the second as soldier – and both for standing their ground while facing adversity. One might say "**bliss copies**" of each other.

The Pursuit of Happiness has a different flair than the previous two sections of our book. Life and Liberty are defined by their counter-weights, death and slavery. The pursuit of happiness lacks such a balancer. **To pursue** can mean **following, chasing, hunting, trailing, tracking, tailing and shadowing**. It can mean **practicing,**

***engaging in, working at, going in for and taking up***. Pursuit is a verb with happiness as a goal. It is Life and Liberty in action.

As action, pursuit demands a pursuer. This is where the body comes into play and becomes practice. In doing so, certain biological systems are activated. **One system is the hypothalamic-pituitary-adrenal (HPA) axis.** A discussion of ameliorating human pain and suffering must engage this axis – and the HPA is modulated by cannabinoids:

> *The present findings demonstrate an important role for endocannabinoid signaling in the process of stress HPA habituation, and suggest that **AEA and 2-AG modulate** different components of the adrenocortical response to repeated stressor exposure.*

Two endocannabinoids, AEA (anandamide) and 2-AG, modulate the HPA axis as it handles stress and pain. Research like the 2010 quote above highlights why cannabinoids are so hot – to people like us and the pharmaceutical companies! They touch every aspect of our health – a point we will continue to develop in this section.

We appreciate pharmaceutical solutions to health problems. Clearly, for those who can afford them, people often enjoy a greater quality of life. Many Americans and their families have benefited personally from prescription drugs. Two major drawbacks for pharmaceuticals, to include synthetic cannabinoids, are side effects and cost.

In the 21$^{st}$ century we are witnessing the *"pharmaceuticalization"* of the pursuit of bliss. Three circumstances seem to account for this momentum: billions invested in research, competition within the industry, and the legal assault on divergent mendicants.

Americans expect advancements in pharmaceuticals, though the sheen of success is waning. There has been too much hype. Prescription drugs, representing billions of dollars in research, development and sales, have become everyday. Millions of people faithfully consume these chemical tools and often experience a better life. Of these pharmaceutical products, entire classes are applied to our mental and emotional functions; the CNS and areas like the HPA axis are main targets. This work is encouraged to search for ever-finer biochemical adjustments of our feelings and well-being – in essence, our happiness.

The deregulation of the pharmaceutical industry is most visible in how and what it advertises. Often the primary plea is for consumers to ask their doctors about the likelihood of a given medicine making them not only well but happier, better looking, and more confident. This pharmaceutical pursuit of happiness is prescription based in its attempt to modulate. Fair enough, though the phrase ***"Life, Liberty and the Prescription for Happiness"*** has never defined the rights of free people.

*The prescription industry's* current situation vis-à-vis cannabis can be summed up by looking at synthetic THC vs. organic THC. Americans can be prescribed Marinol (synthetic THC), a Schedule III drug, for over $60,000 an ounce. Marinol comes in a pill. It is made and sold by a pharmaceutical company. It is delivered by your local pharmacy. On the other side is organic THC from cannabis, a Schedule I drug – meaning the US government argues it has no medical value. In terms of effects and chemistry, the only difference to speak of is that one is manufactured and the other grown. Oh, and one doesn't kill cancer and one does. You will have to ask yourself why this is so – why the one that doesn't kill cancer is legal and costs $60,000 an ounce and the one that kills cancer is a federal felony and costs a couple hundred dollars an ounce. This is only explained by a breakdown of reason.

Keep the scientists named in this book in your thoughts. Think of all the **"et als"** as well. Thousands of names signifying a scientific will to truth reminiscent of Lincoln's *Bliss Copy*.

The larger condition made clear in this war is that we are now living in an age where our emotions are explicitly politicized. The pursuit of happiness is under attack. Experiencing the euphoria of a cannabinoid high can no longer be easily dismissed; it is not giving into temptation, an over-indulgence, a moral flaw, or even a simple kick. Not when questionable promises of joy are being sold to us. Not when organic THC is shown by that same industry's research to positively treat a range of maladies, from pain to depression to cancer. Not when thousands of citizens are being arrested and incarcerated every year for the simple crime of using an herbal cannabinoid to feel, among other things, happy.

Bliss ain't the problem ~ ignorance is.

*Publius*
(2011)

### Search terms

Pursuit of Happiness; hypothalamic-pituitary-adrenal (HPA) axis, anandamide and 2-AG; cannabinoids and vanilloid receptors (TRPV1); synthetic THC (Marinol) vs. organic THC; Lincoln's *Bliss Copy*.

### Research and selected readings

2010: M Pratt-Hyatt, et al, *Effects of a commonly occurring genetic polymorphism of human CYP3A4 (I118V) on the metabolism of anandamide*, Drug Metabolism and Disposition, November 2010:38(11):2075-82.

2010: W Wang, et al, *Deficiency in endocannabinoid signaling in the nucleus accumbens induced by chronic unpredictable stress*, Neuropsychopharmacology, October 2010:35(11):2249-61.

2010: S Eggan, et al, *Cannabinoid CB1 receptor immunoreactivity in the prefrontal cortex: comparison of schizophrenia and major depressive disorder*, September 2010:35(10):2060-71.

2010: B Fonseca, et al, *N-acylethanolamine levels and expression of their metabolizing enzymes during pregnancy*, Endocrinology, August 2010:151(8):3965-74.

2010: S Kozono, et al, *Involvement of the endocannabinoid system in periodontal healing*, Biochemical and Biophysical Research Communications, April 2010:394(4):928-33.

2009: A Toth, et al, *Anandamide and the vanilloid receptor (TRPV1)*, Vitamins and Hormones, 2009:81:389-419.

2009: F Francavilla, et al, *Characterization of the endocannabinoid system in human spermatozoa and involvement of transient receptor potential vanilloid 1 receptor in their fertilizing ability*, Endocrinology, October 2009:150(10):4692-700.

2009: A Straiker and K Mackie, *Cannabinoid signaling in inhibitory autaptic hippocampal neurons*, Neuroscience, September 2009:163(1):190-201.

2009: M Hill, et al, *Chronic stress differentially regulates cannabinoid CB1 receptor binding in distinct hippocampal subfields*, European Journal of Pharmacology, July 2009:614(1-3):66-9.

2008: K Phan, et al, *Cannabinoid modulation of amygdala reactivity to social signals of threat in human*, Neuroscience, March 2008:28(10):2313-9.

2005: A Brizzi, et al, *Design, synthesis, and binding studies of new potent ligands of cannabinoid receptors*, Medicinal Chemistry, November 2005:48(23):7343-50.

1998: E Schlosser, *The prison-industrial complex,* Atlantic Monthly, December.

1986: Translated by Rex Warner, *Plutarch: Fall of the Roman Republic*, Crassus #25-27, Penguin Classics, New York NY.

---

Lady Ella
*I want to be happy*

I want to be happy
But I won't be happy
Till I make you happy, too

Life's really worth giving
When we are mirth-giving
Why can't I give some to you?

When skies are gray
And you say you are blue
I'll send the sun smiling through

I want to be happy
But I won't be happy
Till I make you happy, too

---

#26

## *Lady Ella*, citizenship and cannabis

*Freedom is one of the deepest and noblest aspirations of the human spirit.*

POTUS 40 Reagan

*When I get low I get high.*

Ella Fitzgerald

Ella Fitzgerald, also called *The First Lady of Song* and *Lady Ella*, was awarded the *National Medal of Art* by POTUS 40 Reagan and the *Presidential Medal of Freedom* by POTUS 41 Bush. She collaborated with Dizzy Gillespie, Louis Armstrong, Count Basie and Duke Ellington. She lived an American life and yet was a citizen of the world.

The most innovative of ancient Greek city-states did humanity a favor by creating the status of citizen and the practice of citizenship. Of course, the citizens of antiquity hardly constituted an inclusive class. It wasn't until the last century, after much social struggle and sacrifice, that our predecessors won an application of citizenship closer to universal. When Ella's life started, she had two obstacles blocking her from full voting rights – gender and race. Within her lifetime, both obstacles were legislated away.

When it comes to voting rights, even individuals holding US citizenship can have that right taken away. In all states but Maine, Vermont, and Massachusetts, felons serving time are stripped of their voting rights. In ten states those rights are never reinstated, even after individuals have completed their sentence.

One of these felony offenses at the federal level is the possession and/or the production of cannabis in any amount. Quite a number of prominent elected officials from over the years – our citizen-leaders who are fully participating in the governance of our society – are un-convicted federal cannabis felons. If you ever possessed cannabis, that's a federal felony. It doesn't matter if you were caught – like a line from a movie – *"Convicted? No, never convicted."*

We'll just use their numbers and names to make our point: POTUS 40 Reagan, VPOTUS 41 Quayle, POTUS 42 Clinton, VPOTUS 42 Gore, POTUS 43 Bush, and POTUS 44 Obama.

Aspirants for the highest job in the land are no longer automatically excluded for their past cannabis use. The former Governor of New Mexico and 2012 presidential candidate, Gary Johnson, used medical cannabis to heal a back injury. Though protected by state law, he was in violation of the Controlled Substances Act – making his state use and possession a federal offense. That kind of thinking is absurd as well as harmful.

Let's go to the un-absurd world, the world of science. Here things have to add up or they become trash – tossed on the pile of discredited theories – the pile of *The World is Flat*. Yes, cannabinoids offer a Copernican view of the world – one that is properly placed in science.

The body does not play politics. Biological systems work out their differences and find homeostasis – or they don't. When they don't, we start talking of failed systems: disease. That's the role of cannabinoids: to modulate the workings of other systems and to create homeostasis. Here are a number of the systems modulated:

Skeletal, muscular, circulatory, respiratory, immune,
lymphatic, endocrine, nervous, urinary, digestive,

excretory, reproductive, dopamine, GABA, serotonin, histamine, nicotinic, hypothalamic, pituitary, adrenal …

Cannabinoids influence the headspace of pain and perform vital biological actions such as repairing the blood-brain barrier and remyelinating nerves. Cannabinoids help heal what ails you – to include the root cause of ill health, inflammation:

**STRESS → INFLAMMATION → ILL HEALTH →**
**DISEASE → LOSS OF FUNCTIONING**
**LOSS OF FUNCTIONING =**
**LOSS of *Pursuit of Happiness***

There is a genetic path *away from stress* in the body. It is a sense of well-being, of holding space, of a lived conscious awareness that one's mind, body and entouraging chemicals create the love and highs of life. Love is a high just as happy citizens are high citizens, not low. If a citizen's cannabinoid system isn't able to cope with the stress of modern life by itself, then supplementation is in order. That's what the research and my lived experience suggests. Healthy moods help maintain healthy bodies – and healthy bodies are important for fully-functioning citizens.

Every system is fundamental to our health just like the idea that the well-being of every citizen is fundamental to the good of society. By ending this war we can begin to renew our belief in citizenship. This would be good for cannabinoiders and also for the health of our society as a whole. Peace is the medicine we need now.

*Publius*
*(2011)*

### *Search terms*

Ella Fitzgerald; POTUS pot use; stress, inflammation and cannabinoids; Mauro Maccarrone; Matthew Hill; Daniele Piomelli; cannabinoids and physiology/biology; International Cannabinoid Research Society (ICRS).

### *Research and selected readings*

2011: A Howlett, et al, *Endocannabinoid tone versus constitutive activity of cannabinoid receptors*, British Journal of Pharmacology, 24 March 2011 [Epub].

2010: B Gorzalka and M Hill, *Putative role of endocannabinoid signaling in the etiology of depression and actions of antidepressants*, Progress in Neuro-psychopharmacology & Biological Psychiatry, 24 November 2010 [Epub].

2010: M Maccarrone, *Membrane environment and endocannabinoid signaling*, Frontiers in Physiology, October 2010:1:140.

2010: V Nallendran, et al, *The plasma levels of the endocannabinoid, anandamide, increase with the induction of labour*, BGOB, June 2010:117(7):863-9.

2009: S Gaetani, et al, *The endocannabinoid system as a target for novel anxiolytic and antidepressant drugs*, International Review of Neurobiology, 2009:85:57-72.

2009: M Yates and E Barker, *Organized trafficking of anandamide and related lipids*, Vitamins and Hormones, 2009:81:25-53.

2009: Y Zhao, et al, *Distinct functional and anatomical architecture of the endocannabinoid system in the auditory brainstem*, Neurophysiology, May 2009:101(5):2434-46.

2009: L De Petrocellis, et al, *Chemical synthesis, pharmacological characterization, and possible formation in unicellular fungi of 3-hydroxy-anandamide*, Lipid Research, April 2009:50(4):658-66.

2003: J Sullum, *Saying yes: in defense of drug use*, Tarcher/Putnam, New York NY.

#27

# Omega cannabinoid economics

*Money and an unbalanced diet*

Oil from cannabis seeds, marketed as "Hemp oil," is of high nutritional value because of its 1:3 ratio of Omega-3 to Omega-6 essential fatty acids (EFAs). This perfectly matches the ratio required by the human body.

It is well known that America has a diet problem. The problem is fat – an imbalance of EFAs. Western diets typically have ratios between 1:10 and 1:30. These are dramatically skewed toward Omega-6 and toward imbalance.

Here are the ratios of Omega-3 to Omega-6 in common oils:

| | |
|---|---|
| Cannabis/Hemp | 1:3 |
| Flax | 3:1 |
| Canola | 1:2 |
| Soybean | 1:7 |
| Olive | 1:3–13 |
| Corn | 1:46 |

Oils like cottonseed, grapeseed, peanut and sunflower lack significant amounts of Omega-3.

The corn ratio of 1:46 is the big news here. Publius is pro-corn. It's an amazing plant just like cannabis. Corn's lopsided ratio of

1:46 is the issue and it contributes to our diet problem. American farm policy is pro-corn. The most recent version of the Farm law is the *2008 Food, Conservation and Energy Act.* It subsidizes the growing of corn – the one with the 1:46 ratio. Perhaps in 2013, as this 2008 law is in effect for five years, our President and Congress will consider subsidizing the good oil plant – the one that provides the perfect ratio of 1:3.

***The first step would be to make it legal for American farmers to grow cannabis for oil.*** There would also be a need for investment in equipment, transportation, processing factories, and distribution centers. Sounds like something like this would create jobs. As it stands, the hemp consumed in our country is imported from Canada, China and France.

**Omegas**
**Living Harvest®**
**Tempt™ Hempmilk**

Meet the Good Fats. Have you heard about those great Omega-3's & Omega-6's? Guess what? They're fats! Like their name suggests, these Essential Fatty Acids (EFAs) are required for life. More than any other plant on Earth, hemp seeds provide the perfect balance of naturally-occurring Omega-3's with SDA and Omega-6's with GLA. They have no known allergens, and provide a valuable source of protein, magnesium, phosphorus, vitamin E, iron & zinc.

Hemp oil is special. It has two Omega-3s referred to as DHEA (*docosahexaenoyl ethanolamide*) and EPEA (*eicosapentaenoyl ethanolamide*), which some 2010 research suggests are cancer fighters. They seem to work better than their parent Omega-3 fatty acids, DHA (*docosahexaenoic acid*) and EPA (*eicosapentaenoic acid*). Both showed significant potency when activating ECS receptors.

Omega economics hinge on inflammation. Corn oil is pro-inflammatory: hemp oil is anti-inflammatory. Thus by paying farmers to grow corn, then have that product turned into inflammatory oils that unbalance our diet … well that's nonsensical. It also isn't competitive capitalism.

**Omegas**
**Living Harvest®**

**Hemp seeds – little giants of nutrition**

How did Living Harvest Foods become the #1 hemp foods company? We have more hemp food experience than anyone, always improving our products to bring out the rich, smooth and creamy tastes that only hemp can provide. Hemp is an environmentally-friendly renewable resource that requires neither pesticides nor herbicides. Drinking Tempt™, you'll feel good about nourishing your body and taking care of the planet. We offer a whole line of taste bud-pleasing foods: Tempt Hempmilk, Tempt Frozen Desserts, Organic Hemp Protein and Organic Hemp Oil. Our hemp foods deliver a big taste you won't forget.

*Taste bud-pleasing* – sounds wonderful!

Monetarily, the economics of repealing cannabis prohibition show that there are many politically influential industries: farmers and pharmaceuticals top the list. That's not a conspiracy, only good old economics.

On the other hand, it's bad policy to keep good things from people. That's not the role of government.

Hemp oil, with its one tablespoon of EFAs per day, offers a solution to balancing America's diet. That's a goal worthy of pursuit.

*Publius*
*(2011)*

### Search terms
Compare EFAs in corn vs. cannabis (hemp) oil; *docosahexaenoic acid* (DHA) and *docosahexaenoyl ethanolamide* (DHEA); *eicosapentaenoic acid* (EPA) and *eicosapentaenoyl ethanolamide* (EPEA); Canadian Consortium for the Investigation of Cannabinoids (CCIC); William Courtney; 2008 Food, Conservation and Energy Act.

### Research and selected readings
2011: R Yang, et al, *Decoding functional metabolomics with docosahexaenoyl ethanolamide (DHEA) identifies novel bioactive signals*, Biological Chemistry, 12 July 2011 [Epub].

2010: F Labrie, *DHEA, important source of sex steroids in men and even more in women*, Progress in Brain Research, 2010:182:97-148.

2010: T Bisogno and V Di Marzo, *Cannabinoid receptors and endocannabinoids: role in neuroinflammatory and neurodegenerative disorders*, CNS & Neurological Disorders Drug Targets, November 2010:9(5):564-73.

2010: M Balvers, et al, *Docosahexaenoic acid and eicosapentaenoic acid are converted by 3T3-L1 adipocytes to N-acylethanolamines with anti-inflammatory properties*, Biochemical and Biophysical, October 2010:1801(10):1107-14.

2010: K Birnie, et al, *Psychological benefits for cancer patients and their partners participating in mindfulness-based [yoga] stress reduction (MBSR)*, Psycho-oncology, September 2010:19(9):1004-9.

2010: I Brown, et al, *Cannabinoid receptor-dependent and -independent anti-proliferative effects of omega-3 ethanolamides in androgen receptor-positive and -negative prostrate cancer cell lines*, Carcinogenesis, September 2010:31(9):1584-91.

2010: F Massa, et al, *Alterations in the hippocampal endocannabinoid system in diet-induced obese mice*, Neuroscience, May 2010:30(18):6273-81.

2009: D Hoffman, et al, *Toward optimizing vision and cognition in term infants by dietary DHA and ARA supplementation: a review of randomized controlled trials*, Prostaglandins, Leukotrienes and Essential Fatty Acids, Aug-Sep 2009:81(2-3):151-8.

2008: M Radwan, et al, *Non-cannabinoid constituents from a high potency cannabis sativa variety*, Phytochemistry, October 2008:69(14):2627-33.

2007: D Boudreaux, *The politics of prohibition*, Reason, 31 July 2007.

2005: J Miron, *The budgetary implications of marijuana prohibition*, MPP, June 2005.

2003: N Auestad, et al, *Visual, cognitive, and language assessments at 39 months: a follow-up study of children fed formulas containing long-chain polyunsaturated fatty acids to 1 year of age*, Pediatrics, September 2003:112(3 Pt 1):e17783.

2002: A Simopoulos, *Omega-3 fatty acids in inflammation and autoimmune diseases*, American College of Nutrition, December 2002:21(6):495-505.

1995: T Smart, *Other therapies for wasting*, GMHC Treatment Issues, May 1995:9(5):7-8, 12.

#28

# Acetaminophen's CS connection

*Mom talks pain with Publius*

**Publius:** Hey mom?

**Mom:** Yeah.

**Publius:** What do you know about acetaminophen?

**Mom:** You mean Tylenol?

**Publius:** Right.

**Mom:** It's a pain reliever. It works well. – What's to know?

**Publius:** Any problems?

**Mom:** Sure – you're not supposed to take too many of them or drink alcohol. I remember you taking them for hangovers.

**Publius:** Nice one. That was awhile ago though – and aspirin usually worked better for me.

**Mom:** So what's to know about acetaminophen?

**Publius:** It's this research title – *Conversion of acetaminophen to the bioactive N-acylphenolamine AM404 via fatty acid amide hydrolase-dependent arachidonic acid conjugation in the nervous system.*

**Mom:** Acetaminophen and arachidonic acid together? Arachidonic acid is Omega-6, right?

**Publius:** Yes.

**Mom:** Well, that is interesting. That would make Tylenol … a friend of cannabinoids?

**Publius:** Yes …through our ECS.

**Mom:** Why refer to it as *"endo"* anymore. No one talks about their *Endo-digestive system*, do they?

**Publius:** No, you're right.

**Mom:** So just call it CS then … I can't wait to tell your Aunt Mary she's been taking a cannabinoid drug all these years!

**Publius:** Or her kids …

**Mom:** That's more common than you think. I've done that – given children acetaminophen for sleep modification.

**Publius:** We won't keep going over the numbers, but the fact that cannabis prohibition has incarcerated millions of non-violent citizens is just wrong. Then to know that mothers are giving their children a mainstream CS medication – that's just weird.

**Mom:** Deviants.

**Publius:** What's that?

**Mom:** Deviancy – pot's always been deviant. It was bad, you know, to even touch the stuff. It was like one puff would drive you insane.

**Publius:** That's the movie Reefer Madness.

**Mom:** It is? I never saw that – only heard about it.

**Publius:** Have you heard of *Clinical Endocannabinoid Deficiency – CECD*.

**Mom:** Hey there's the endo –

**Publius:** That's right!

**Mom:** So it means their CS isn't working properly.

**Publius:** Right. Lots of my friends complain of an **Exo-**cannabinoid deficiency.

**Mom:** Out of pot …right?

**Publius:** Right on!

**Mom:** Still find yourself amusing, don't you?

**Publius:** Mostly.

**Mom:** It seems like prohibition's business is to produce violence in our communities – that's because the war on cannabis makes it so expensive. It's basic capitalism: mess with supply and demand by making something wanted illegal and watch the price skyrocket.

**Publius:** So they should ban acetaminophen and make millions!

**Mom:** Right, start arresting mothers! Make giving Tylenol to a child a felony and let's build some prisons.

**Publius:** Oh-oh.

**Mom:** What?

**Publius:** You're really getting into this.

**Mom:** I've seen enough to know a few things. Like the taxpayer is also a scarcely mentioned victim in this war. They are the one's funding the cannabis wars – as well as losing out on possible revenue from taxing cannabis.

**Publius:** True.

**Mom:** What were you saying about cannabinoids and Tylenol – how's it work?

**Publius:** Well, it is also known as *Paracetamol* and it modulates the CS. It does so by engaging the CB1 receptor, suggesting its pain-relieving action is modulated by the body's cannabinoid system.

**Mom:** And that is what aspirin does as well?

**Publius:** Pretty much – aspirin and this group are referred to as *NSAIDs* – nonsteroidal anti-inflammatory drugs. Even simple things like Echinacea activate cannabinoid receptors.

**Mom:** Fascinatingly pain-free stuff P.

**Publius:** Thanks mom.

*Publius*
*(2011)*

**Search terms**
Paracetamol/Acetaminophen; anandamide, CS and pain relief; emergency room visits for acetaminophen; NSAIDs; CS and cyclooxygenases inhibitors; Tylenol, Echinacea and cannabinoid receptors.

**Research and selected readings**
2011: *New cannabinoid laws ban common products*, Retail Compliance Association press release, 20 June.

2011: H Paunescu, et al, *Cannabinoid system and cyclooxygenases inhibitors*, Medicine and Life, Jan-Mar 2011:4(1):11-20.

2010: I Kubajewska and C Constantinescu, *Cannabinoids and experimental models of multiple sclerosis*, Immunobiology, August 2010:215(8):647-57.

2008: M Egger, et al, *Synthesis and cannabinoid receptor activity of ketoalkenes from Echinacea pallida and nonnatural analogues*, Chemistry, 2008:14(35):10978-84.

2008: C Mallet, et al, *Endocannabinoid and serotonergic systems are needed for acetaminophen-induced analgesia*, Pain, September 2008:139(1):190-200.

2008: M Cupini, et al, *Degradation of endocannabinoids in chronic migraine and medication overuse headache*, Neurobiology of Disease, May 2008:30(2):186-9.

2008: E Russo, *Clinical endocannabinoid deficiency (CECD): can this concept explain therapeutic benefits of cannabis in migraine, fibromyalgia, irritable bowel syndrome and other treatment-resistant conditions?* Neuro Endocrinology Letters, April 2008:29(2):192-200.

2006: S Raduner, et al, *Alkymides from Echinacea are a new class of cannabinomimetics: cannabinoid type 2 receptor-dependent and –independent immunomodulatory effects*, Biological Chemistry, May 2006:281(20):14192-206.

2006: A Ottani, et al, *The analgesic activity of Paracetamol is prevented by the blockade of cannabinoid CB1 receptors*, European Journal of Pharmacology, February 2006:531(1-3):280-1.

2005: D Hogstatt, et al, *Conversion of acetaminophen to the bioactive N-acylphenolamine AM404 via fatty acid amide hydrolase-dependent arachidonic acid conjugation in the nervous system*, Biological Chemistry, September 2005:280(36):31405-12.

1988: P Harvison, et al, *Acetaminophen as a cosubstrate and inhibitor of prostaglandin H synthase*, Chemico-biological Interactions, 1988:64(3):251-66.

*Who is Shadow?*

*Shadow lurks in fear, rearing a cloaked, ignorant head when change is in the air. This time "He" appears in the news in dark shadow, giving himself the name of Joe ... Joe Doe. His speech is incoherent and innocuous. I too was under the spell of Shadow. I was trying to be anonymous – trying to blend in with everyone else – until I heard story upon story of my fellow citizens suffering in pain, and living without the relief of an elixir called cannabis. There was only one thing to do – that was to break Shadow's spell. I vowed to never again wear that ignorant cloak because it weakened my powers like kryptonite. I'd rather be seen and heard in the light of truth, justice and cannabinoids for those who want them – and in doing so, to help humankind heal the earth.*

*Unknown*

#29

# Cannabinoids throw up a conundrum

*Dad talks of nicotine, serotonin and emesis with Publius*

**Publius:** Thanks for meeting me in the pub.

**Dad:** My pleasure.

**Publius:** This place would be better if we could supplement our CS.

**Dad:** You mean "*Skin up*" right here?

**Publius:** Skin up?

**Dad:** You don't know that one? When I was in London tending bar at a pub that's what they called rolling-up a joint.

**Publius:** They?

**Dad:** Oh yeah – that was an interesting time in my life.

**Publius:** I'm sure it was – tell me more. Where did you work?

**Dad:** *The Cornwallis* pub named after Lord Charles Cornwallis, the general who surrendered to Washington at Yorktown. Working there was a perpetual cycle of intoxication.

**Publius:** Really?

**Dad:** Well, customers didn't tip bartenders, but they did buy them drinks. So, during my shift I would have a few drinks, and then some cola to stay sharp, and maybe a couple drinks after work. To unwind a little more when we got back to our apartment, we **skinned up**. Buds were hard to get, so we crushed hashish into a tobacco cigarette. It helped us unwind after just getting off a long day of work. Then you had to get up and clean the pub the next morning. Before the morning shift, we would **skin up** again to deal with the increasingly apparent hangover.

**Publius:** Interesting dad – that is a perpetual cycle of intoxication, or you could look at it another way. You said before that you smoked cigarettes.

**Dad:** Yup – for several years. Then quit one day. It was easier for me than most people. It really grabs some friends of mine.

**Publius:** That makes sense.

**Dad:** Why?

**Publius:** Nicotine has a receptor. That makes it a modulator of consciousness. It also means we would have genetic differences as to its effect on the body. Some people would be genetically wired to be more inclined to its effects. Some would need it.

**Dad:** Why would someone **need** nicotine?

**Publius:** I know – it's an odd thought – though if there is a receptor there is an **endo** for it.

**Dad:** I get it – like how they found anandamide.

**Publius:** Right. The ***endo*** for nicotine is ***acetylcholine.***

**Dad:** I didn't know that.

**Publius:** It does a lot. It can be both an agonist and antagonist. It inhibits and excites. In our nervous system the endo is a modulator of cell signaling and effects arousal and reward.

**Dad:** Sex and the smoke break.

**Publius:** Right. In *TCP* we discuss products that mimic cannabinoid activity. It's legal to market and purchase appetite supplements and baby food that are intended to boost cannabinoid activity.

**Dad:** Neat. I'm still stuck at the idea that nicotine has a receptor. That's interesting P.

**Publius:** It's an old receptor too. It shares characteristics with the 5HT receptors.

**Dad:** What are they?

**Publius:** Serotonin. One in particular, the 5HT3 receptor –

**Dad:** That doesn't help.

**Publius:** It's the emesis receptor and cannabinoids modulate it.

**Dad:** *Emesis?*

**Publius:** Throwing up, puking.

**Dad:** Oh right, like at the *Cornwallis*.

**Publius:** Takes ya back?

**Dad:** You got a message on your phone.

**Publius:** Okay . . . looks like you've been saved from an emesis story.

**Dad:** Time for you to get going?

**Publius:** Right – my ride's here.

**Dad:** Well have a good one – and don't forget to Skin up!

**Publius:** I'll remember! Thanks dad.

*Publius*
*(2011)*

### Search terms
Serotonin, 5HT receptors and cannabinoids; acetylcholine, nicotinic receptors, nicotine, niacinamide, and nicotinamide.

### Research and selected readings
2011: S Haj-Dahmane and R Shen, *Modulation of the serotonin system by endocannabinoid signaling*, Neuropharmacology, September 2011:61(3):414-20 [Epub].

2011: C Mannucci, et al, *Interactions between endocannabinoid and serotonergic systems in mood disorders caused by nicotine withdrawal*, Nicotine and Tobacco Research, April 2011:13(4):239-47.

2010: L Parker, et al, *Regulation of nausea and vomiting by cannabinoids*, British Journal of Pharmacology, 22 December 2010 [Epub].

2010: K Yang, et al, *The effect of Δ9-tetrahydrocannabinol on 5-HT3 receptors depends on the current density*, Neuroscience, November 2010:171(1):40-9.

2010: G Muccioli, et al, *The endocannabinoid system links to gut microbiota and adipogenesis*, Molecular Systems Biology, July 2010:6:392.

2010: M Oz, et al, *The endogenous cannabinoid, anandamide, inhibits dopamine transporter function by a receptor-independent mechanism*, Neurochemistry, March 2010:112(6):1454-64.

2007: S Batkai, et al, *Cannabinoid-2 receptor mediates protection against hepatic ischemia/reperfusion injury*, FASBE Journal, June 2007:21(8):1788-800.

2002: D Townsend, et al, *Cannabinoids throw up a conundrum*, British Journal of Pharmacology, November 2002:137(5):575-7.

2001: C Ratsch, *Marijuana medicine: a world tour of the healing and visionary powers of cannabis,* Healing Arts Press, Rochester VT.

2000: G Kunos, et al, *Endocannabinoids as cardiovascular modulators*, Chemistry and Physics of Lipids, November 2000:108(1-2):159-68.

1999: J Cheer, et al, *Modification of 5-HT2 receptor mediated behaviour in the rat by oleamide and the role of cannabinoid receptors*, Neuropharmacology, April 1999:38(4):533-41.

1995: P Fan, *Cannabinoid agonists inhibit the activation of 5-HT3 receptors in rat nodose ganglion neurons*, Neurophysiology, February 1995:73(2):907-10.

---

*Staying positive in a negative world.*

*Displaced energy and retrograde signaling.*

*We enjoy a joint to calm ourselves down –
to end the negative energy –
and let it go.*

---

#30

## Intimate amygdala action *pot*entials

*Since the amygdala is believed to be a neuronal circuit
of emotional memories …*

Kodirov, et al (2009)

I've worked in construction most of my life – constructing impenetrable walls inside myself.

Life can flow like a beautifully orchestrated piece of music. As we live and pursue happiness, the music becomes more complex. The violins may get out-of-synch with the cellos, leaving the group wondering how to regain a unified rhythm. Sometimes I used to feel like a conductor who uses every ounce of energy to pull the orchestra together, even though that over-stressed conductor knows the percussion section lost its sense of timing years ago.

You see, I've always thought of myself as a strong and independent person. Since acquiring an illness, those qualities became more prominent in my day-to-day life. I took to managing illness with *Jackson-Pollack-fervor*. I would swirl mortar on to walls with a flick of consciousness. My life became filled with pharmaceuticals, dietary supplements, mobility devices, and human services. This allowed me to live in a modified apartment, drive a modified car, and work a modified schedule. I began to live a modified life – not a "modulated" one.

---

### *"The CS Modulation Orchestra"*
*Score 1, Action Potentials*
*Kodirov, et al (2009)*

1. The ***amygdala*** is a key area of the brain where the emotional memories are stored throughout the lifespan.

2. Pavlovian classical conditioning is accompanied by an increase in synaptic strength within ***the fear circuit*** of the amygdala.

3. However, a type of short-term synaptic plasticity, known as ***depolarization-induced suppression of excitation (DSE)***, has not been studied previously in the amygdala.

4. DSE, similar to depolarization-induced suppression of inhibition (DSI), ***recruits a cross talk*** between pre- and postsynaptic neurons.

5. The suppression can be achieved not only by depolarization of the postsynaptic neuron, but also by brief trains of ***action potentials (APs)*** evoked by stimulation of innervating fibers.

---

Prior to using cannabis it was extremely difficult for me to ask for help. It wasn't just a bother; it had reached the level of problem because it kept reinforcing those impenetrable walls. Just like any habit, I started looping. There I was always trying to accept the past and the present all at once. I didn't want to trouble anyone or have them feeling sorry for me. A sardonic voice became part of my internal dialogue:

*"No! Don't feel sorry for me! I can do it myself! Even though my legs are slowly failing me, let me show you how much I can still do! I'm not embarrassed that I just fell because I had to prove I could pick up those dropped keys by my feet – I am still worthy!"*

Of course, I wasn't feeling worthy and fiercely kept up the façade. This habit included the desire to paint the rosiest picture I could – *"Everything's fine!"* I would say to whoever was listening. Then one day I realized I was saying it more for me than them.

Cannabinoids helped me get there. Now I know how to relax – how that feels again. When I'm relaxed I can ask for help. I started deconstructing emotional memories and the walls of pride and ego. I began to understand "asking" as a healing modality – as an entourage power. As I asked I opened myself up to others, then the healing arrived. I found power – *my power* – in asking others for help.

The CS is not magic; it offers the power of cannabinoids to one's self – then change begins. Asking and being open became a new language for me. Initially, every time I asked for help, I would momentarily feel awkward and uncertain – as if I had just mispronounced a word or hit the wrong note. The asking got easier the more I practiced.

---

### The CS Modulation Orchestra
*Score 2, Multiple Receptors*
*Kodirov, et al (2009)*

Here we show four different kinds of receptors modulated by cannabinoids and their entouraging ligands. This allows retrograde transmission initiated by the ***action potentials*** in the postsynaptic pyramidal neuron:

1.  ***AMPA***,   α-amino-3-hydroxy-5-methyl-4-isoxazolepropionic acid glutamate ***receptor***

2.  ***GABA***, γ-aminobutyric acid ***receptor***

3.  ***NMDA***, *N*-methyl-D-aspartate glutamate ***receptor***

4.  ***CB1***, cannabinoid ***receptor*** type 1

5.  ***eCB***, endogenous ***cannabinoid ligands***

---

Practice I did. I started speaking out to whoever would listen about the noticeable changes cannabis was having on my body, mind and soul. I intimately talked about my failing mobility, depressed head, leaking bladder and bowels. That's pretty intimate. I had to get comfortable quick if I was going to share my salvation story. I had intimate conversations with everyone – from neighbors to state and federal legislators. I allowed intimacy into my living room by conversing with news reporters and camera crews. There I was telling them all about my personal plumbing and mental states while sitting at the kitchen table.

My CS allowed me to break down the walls inside myself – the one's I had constructed. I could relate differently, more intimately, to everyone – making connections instead of building walls.

---

### The CS Modulation Orchestra
*Score 3, DSE in LA*
*Kodirov, et al (2009)*

1.  The ***lateral amygdala (LA) is modulated*** by excitatory afferents and involved in synaptic plasticity, i.e., the counterpart that underlies learning and memory at neuronal level.

2.  Our results demonstrate that DSE is present in a majority of LA pyramidal neurons. Further experiments reveal endogenous ***cannabinoids as the messengers for this retrograde signaling*** in the LA.

3.  This is an important observation since ***the density of cannabinoid receptors in the amygdala is relatively high***; and even higher in a human compared to a rat.

4.  At this time, we are not aware of ***any other modulators*** and/or third messengers (other than endocannabinoids) responsible for the retrograde signaling in the LA.

5.  In conclusion, to our knowledge, this is the ***first successful attempt to show DSE in the LA*** that improves our understanding of the physiological impact of the $CB_1R$ and its ligand(s) in this center.

---

It's important to remember our sense of self is invested in intimacy. **That's the risk.** It's why being open to others causes so much fear. It takes effort to change your perspective on your body and life – like going from not having MS to having it.

Time is a commodity filled with potential. There is always something to do – even nothing! Time is also a common theme among friends I share cannabis with. It doesn't seem to matter if they are relatives, coworkers, or even new acquaintances; we all need time to think. Cannabis brings people together – sometimes by showing us we're not really that far apart.

The CS is a remarkable part of our every day. It brought me closer to people. It enhances intimacy – which then makes things like openness, friendship and love possible. Cannabis doesn't necessarily destroy the walls we've created. What it does is allow one to create doors and open windows within those walls. That changes everything.

~~~~~~~~

This piece was performed by the intimate words of One accompanied by *"The CS Modulation Orchestra"* and the science of Kodirov, et al.

We are all One: for this presentation "the One" was a woman with Multiple Sclerosis. The three Kodirov Scores echo and explain the relationship between her emotional memories and ***action potentials.*** In the first Score we learned that "the One" stores her emotional memories in the ***amygdala***. Score 2 directed us to ***four kinds of receptors***, AMPA, GABA, NMDA, and CB1, as well as to other key endocannabinoid activity. Score 3 reminds us of the importance of cannabinoids as ***retrograde messengers*** and their effect on ***action potentials***.

*Publius*
*(2011)*

### Search terms
DSE; amygdala cannabinoid receptors; action potentials; Vincenzo Di Marzo; Luciano De Petrocellis.

### Research and selected readings
2011: T Ohno-Shosaku, et al, *Endocannabinoids and retrograde modulation of synaptic transmission*, Neuroscientist, 29 April 2011 [Epub].

2011: F Gilli, et al, *Loss of braking signal during inflammation: a factor affecting the development and disease course of multiple sclerosis*, Archives of Neurology, 14 March 2011 [Epub].

2011: A Hariri and P Whalen, *The amygdala: inside and out*, F1000 Biology Reports, January 2011:3:2.
~~~~~~~~

2009: S Kodirov, et al, *Endogenous cannabinoids trigger the depolarized-induced suppression of excitation (DSE) in the lateral amygdala*, Learning & Memory, December 2009:17(1):43-9.

2009: M Zhang, et al, *Modulation of cannabinoid receptor activation as a neuroprotective strategy for EAE and stroke*, Neuroimmune Pharmacology, June 2009:4(2):249-59.

2007: C Streeter, et al, *Yoga Asana sessions increase brain GABA levels: a pilot study,* Alternative and Complementary Medicine, May 2007:13(4):419-26.

2005: R Bergner, *I smoke pot with my family: speaking up at 85*, iUniverse, New York NY.

2004: M Diana and A Marty, *Endocannabinoid-mediated short-term synaptic activity: depolarized-induced suppression of inhibition (DSI) and depolarized-induced suppression of excitation (DSE)*, British Journal of Pharmacology, May 2004:142(1):9-19.

2003: D Ford, *Good medicine, great sex!* Good Press, Sonoma CA.

2003: S Brown, et al, *Brief presynaptic bursts evoke synapse-specific retrograde inhibition mediated by endogenous cannabinoids*, Nature Neuroscience, October 2003:6(10):1048-57.

2002: T Ohno-Shosaku, et al, *Presynaptic cannabinoid sensitivity is a major determinant of depolarized-induced retrograde suppression of hippocampal synapses*, Neuroscience, May 2002:22(10):3864-72.

---

*Muddy Waters*
*Champagne & Reefer*

Yeah bring me champagne when I'm thirsty.
Bring me reefer when I want to get high.
Yeah bring me champagne when I'm thirsty.
Bring me reefer when I want to get high.
Well you know when I'm lonely
Bring my woman set her right down here by my side.
Well you know there should be no law
on people that want to smoke a little dope.
Well you know there should be no law
on people that want to smoke a little dope.
Well you know it's good for your head
And it relax your body don't you know.

Everytime I get high
I lay my head down on my baby's breast.
Well you know I lay down be quiet
Tryin' to take my rest.
Well you know she done hug and kiss me
Says Muddy you're one man that I love the best.

I'm gonna get high
Gonna get high just as sure as you know my name.
Y'know I'm gonna get so high this morning
It's going to be a cryin' shame.
Well you know I'm gonna stick with my reefer
Ain't gonna be messin' round with no cocaine.

---

#31

# Drugism/Racism

*We were born into the drug war the way slaves were born into slavery.*

Publius

**Drugism**

In Michelle Alexander's *The New Jim Crow*, we are shown a vision of America's new form of discrimination as understood through the "felon":

> What has changed since the collapse of Jim Crow has less to do with the basic structure of our society than with the language we use to justify it. In the era of colorblindness, it is no longer socially permissible to use race, explicitly, as a justification for discrimination, exclusion, and social contempt. So we don't. Rather than rely on race, we use our criminal justice to label people of color "criminals" and then engage in all the practices we supposedly left behind. Today it is perfectly legal to discriminate against criminals in nearly all ways that it was once legal to discriminate against African-Americans. ***Once you're labeled a felon, the old forms of discrimination – employment***

> **discrimination, housing discrimination, denial of the right to vote, denial of educational opportunity, denial of food stamps and other public benefits, and exclusion from jury service – are suddenly legal.** As a criminal, you have scarcely more rights, and arguably less respect, than a black man living in Alabama at the height of Jim Crow.

At the opening of this essay we quoted something that we kept saying at our meetings: *We were born into the drug war the way slaves were born into slavery.* Then when Alexander's book was published in 2009, she provided the theoretical framework for what we were feeling – the concept of "drugism."

If you think pot causes cancer or if you believe using cannabis makes you dumb – those are drugisms. They are ideas that thrive on myth-making and stereotypes. They are easy to use (convenient even) because they support things that people want to believe – like people who use drugs are bad. That can't be true though in a nation where pharmaceutical sales topped $300 billion last year: that, my friends, is drugism par excellence.

In terms of the pursuit of happiness, people who consume cannabis are overwhelmingly peaceful when compared to the violent effect of other legal and illegal drugs. Cannabis culture has continued its pursuit of happiness for personal, spiritual or medical reasons regardless of the rule of law. Although arrests continue to rise, science and awareness favor cannabis. Ending America's draconian laws represents a shift in this transformation. We can expect the conflict between two truths, the 800,000 arrests versus the cannabinoid system, to reveal itself in the near future on a multitude of social and legal fronts.

**Racism**

Cordelia Stevenson lived near Columbus, Mississippi. She was the mother of a son suspected of wrongdoing. It was during the time when mobs lynched people:

Once having settled on lynch justice, mobs were not overly scrupulous about determining the guilt of the black victim. The idea, after all, as one black observer noted, was to make an example, *"knowing full well that one Negro swinging from a tree will serve as well as another to terrorize the community."* After a barn burning near Columbus, Mississippi, suspicion fell on the son of Cordelia Stevenson. Unable to locate him, a mob of whites settled on his mother, seized and tortured her, and left her naked body hanging from the limb of a tree for public viewing. A jury rendered the usual judgment in such cases, deciding she had come to her death **at the hands of persons unknown**.

Terror overwhelms with our fear of helplessness. We discuss the deaths of three citizens in this book. These three faced impossible situations and preventable deaths. *Jonathan Magbie* died in the custody of local law enforcement; *Robin Prosser* died in fear of federal custody; *Cordelia Stevenson* died in the custody of her community. All three died with fellow citizens watching and in place to protect them. Anyone could have yelled something like – ***"Stop! This is wrong!"*** That might have made someone else think the same thing. Sometimes that's all it takes to stop evil. One person speaking out when it is most needed. It's courage in the face of adversity.

Magbie, Prosser or Stevenson did not commit a crime worthy of being denied compassion. They also did not die **"at the hands of persons unknown."** People knew these citizens needed relief. Compassion is not a difficult morality to exhibit. It means helping those in need. Magbie, Prosser and Stevenson were all in need of protection from their fellow citizens. No one offered respite or relief. No one helped them in their need on the day they died. In real terms, one can't imagine another's thoughts at the moment of death. One can imagine feelings like the *ensconcing terror of helplessness* and the *determining horror of hopelessness* and feel empathy for their last moments. Traditionally, compassion has been a higher human feeling valued as exceptional.

What is the effect on us when we accept the arresting of 800,000 Americans for herbal cannabinoids? Perhaps arresting citizens for plant crimes is not good government.

That depends though: as Alexander points out – all those felons are serving more than time; they are serving a purpose as well.

Young black men are a large part of the 800,000 arrests. So are other minorities. It's easy to imagine there are plenty of would-be Dizzy Gillespies, Cab Calloways, and Barry Obamas being arrested.

When you look at the history of racism you immediately see the language games it involves – which leads you to see how changing the language has changed racism. We haven't ended racism and won't. It is the effects that are changing. Power now uses the felon to discriminate. When you look at the effects of racism in the context of 70 years of cannabis prohibition, it is clear that something wrong is taking place. Racism is a component of drugism and it is complicit in keeping citizens from helping other citizens. We end up calling it things like "class war" or want to place the blame on capitalism. Instead, isn't it our policies that divide – and not us? I will not waste another generation in this war. No more failing. The CS is fundamental to one's health: arresting someone for supplementing their CS – that's criminal.

Cannabinoids seem to be the least discriminating substance shared by humans. An *–ism* blinds one to another's reality. We are the ones who allow others to wage war on our own citizens. The plant offers healing. Maybe we should do the same.

The denial of *Life, Liberty and the Pursuit of Happiness* is not an American tradition worth supporting. Less needless helplessness and more compassion – that would be a better tradition.

*Publius*
(2011)

**Search terms**
Cordelia Stevenson; potent ligands of cannabinoid receptors; therapeutic potential of cannabinoids; Jim Crow laws; Harlem Hamfats; Medgar Evers; Crucial Conflict.

**Research and selected readings**
2011: H Tan, et al, *Cannabinoid transmission in the basolateral amygdala modulates fear memory formation via functional inputs to the prelimbic cortex*, Neuroscience, April 2011:31(14):5300-12.

2011: T Esch and G Stefano, *The neurobiological link between compassion and love*, Medical Science Monitor, February 2011:17(3):RA65-75.

2010: P Mukhopadhyay, et al, *Cannabinoid-2 receptor limits inflammation, oxidative/nitrosative stress, and cell death in nephropathy*, Free Radical Biology & Medicine, February 2010:48(3):457-67.

2009: M Alexander, *The new Jim Crow: mass incarceration in the age of colorblindness*, The New Press, New York NY.

2009: M Zhang, et al, *CB2 receptor activation attenuates microcirculatory dysfunction during cerebral ischemic/reperfusion injury*, Microvascular Research, June 2009:78(1):86-94.

2005: A Brizzi, et al, *Design, synthesis, and binding studies of new potent ligands of cannabinoid receptors*, Medicinal Chemistry, November 2005:48(23):7343-50.

2005: R Melamede, *Harm reduction – the cannabis paradox*, Harm Reduction Journal, September 2005:2:17.

2003: J Croxford, *Therapeutic potential of cannabinoids in CNS disease*, CNS Drugs, 2003:17(3):179-202.

2000: J Allen, et al, *Without sanctuary: lynching photography in America*, Twin Palms Publishers, Santa Fe NM.

2000: S Watson, et al, *Marijuana and medicine: assessing the science base: a summary of the 1999 Institute of Medicine report*, Archives of General Psychiatry, June 2000:57(6):547-52.

1995: R Doblin and M Kleiman, *The medical use of marijuana: the case for clinical trials*, Addictive Diseases, 1995:14(1):5-14.

#32

# Respecting cannabis respects nature

*"Hippies can't stand death metal."*

*South Park's Cartman*

The Illinois Constitution, Section 1 of the Bill of Rights states:

> "All men are by nature free and independent and have certain inherent and inalienable rights among which are **life, liberty and the pursuit of happiness**."

Those aren't hippy words, though they are constitutional words hippies would applaud. We talked a lot about music and cannabis in this book. We've also discussed how cannabis kills cancer. We haven't said much about the myth that cannabis smoking *causes* cancer. It's a myth. A 2009 US government funded study tried to prove the myth true and failed. The study examined the frequency of heavy cannabis smokers and lung cancer. The study showed a negative correlation between cannabis smoking and lung cancer, not a positive one. The research ended up implying cannabis smokers might be protecting their lungs from cancer, which is consistent with other cannabinoid and cancer research.

We mention that in order to talk about things used to discredit cannabis. The media likes to show pictures of joint smoking rockers.

That's because rock-n-roll and cannabis prohibition share a common heritage. They also share another characteristic: ***the ability to entourage***.

Sure, music and cannabinoids can be "used" independently of the group. It's just that the two go better with others.

There's a somewhat famous song that captures the essence of our culture's relationship to cannabis. Black Sabbath, a pioneer of heavy metal and forerunner of death metal, praises cannabis in *Sweet Leaf*:

*ALRIGHT NOW!*
*Won't you listen?*

*When I first met you, didn't realize*
*I can't forget you, for your surprise*
*you introduced me, to my mind*
*And left me wanting, you and your kind*

*I love you, Oh you know it*

*My life was empty, forever on a down*
*Until you took me, showed me around*
*My life is free now, my life is clear*
*I love you sweet leaf, though you can't hear*

*Come on now, try it out*

*Straight people don't know, what you're about*
*They put you down and shut you out*
*you gave to me a new belief*
*and soon the world will love you sweet leaf*

Cannabinoids, like bands, work better when entouraging. Two examples of entouragers (also referred to as congeners) are *oleoylethanolamide* (OEA) and *palmitoylethanolamide* (PEA), though all cannabinoids entourage. One entourager of little notice is *stearoylethanolamide (SEA)*. In 2002 it was reported to be in mammalian brains at comparable levels with anandamide. In 2008 research, SEA was hailed for its "promising therapeutic benefit in reducing allergic inflammation in the skin." By 2010, the white-coats were investigating SEA's cannabimimetic actions in diseased brains.

Cartman may be correct that hippies can't stand death metal. Some hippies don't even like classic Black Sabbath. There is that one song though, *Paranoid,* that hippies get. – Oh yeah, we understand that one.

I suppose music is like most things in life – it doesn't matter if you are straight, hippy, or metalhead – you just might end up sharing a cannabinoid high with someone … and some admiration for the *Sweet Leaf.*

*Publius*
*(2011)*

### Search terms
South Park's "Die Hippie, Die"; Black Sabbath's *Sweet Leaf;* *oleoylethanolamide* (OEA), *palmitoylethanolamide* (PEA), *linoleoylethanolamide* (LEA), and *stearoylethanolamide* (SEA); IDOC Jason Spyres #K99397.

### Research and selected readings
2011: D Vara, et al, *Anti-tumoral action of cannabinoids on hepatocellular carcinoma: role of AMPK-dependent activation of autophagy,* Cell Death and Differentiation, April 2011 [Epub].

2010: H Hansen, *Palmitoylethanolamide and other anandamide congeners: proposed role in the diseased brain,* Experimental Neurology, July 2010:224(1):48-55.

2009: H Hansen and T Diep, *N-acylethanolamines, anandamide and food intake,* Biochemical Pharmacology, September 2009:78(6):553-60.

2009: D Tashkin, *Does smoking marijuana increase the risk of chronic obstructive pulmonary disease?* CMAJ, April 2009:180(8):797-8.

2008: W Ho, et al, *'Entourage' effects of N-palmitoylethanolamide and N-oleoylethanolamide on vasorelaxation to anandamide occur through TRPV1 receptors*, British Journal of Pharmacology, November 2008:155(6):837-46.

2008: M Dalle Carbonare, et al, *A saturated N-acylethanolamine other than N-palmitoyl ethanolamine with anti-inflammatory properties: a neglected story...*, Neuroendocrinology, May 2008:20 Suppl 1:26-34.

2007: E Dainese, et al, *Modulation of the endocannabinoid system by lipid rafts*, Current Medicinal Chemistry, 2007:14(25):2702-15.

2006: M Bari, et al, *Effect of lipid rafts on CB2 receptor signaling and 2-arachidonoyl-glycerol metabolism in human immune cells*, Immunology, October 2006:177(8):4971-80.

2005: B Venables, et al, *N-acylethanolamines in seeds of selected legumes*, Phytochemistry, August 2005:66(16):1913-8.

2002: M Maccarrone, et al, *Binding, degradation and apoptotic activity of stearoylethanolamide in rat C6 glioma cells*, Biochemical, August 2002:366(Pt 1):137-44.

1999: D Lambert and V Di Marzo, *The palmitoylethanolamide and oleamide enigmas: are these two fatty acid amides cannabimimetic?* Current Medicinal Chemistry, August 1999:6(8):757-73.

#33

# *CB3 it is!* – reproducing revolutions

*Cannabinoids and a newly discovered receptor*

We've been researching, writing and publishing this collection of essays for about six years. While learning about CB1 and CB2 receptors, we noticed that many researchers were hypothesizing a third receptor – ***a CB3 receptor***. Then in the last month of work, in June 2011, this article appeared on PubMed: *Modulation of the novel cannabinoid receptor – **GPR55** – during rat fetoplacental development*.

That's the research reporting discovery of the elusive CB3, referred to as *GPR55*. That will add clarity and open up new hypotheses concerning cannabinoids.

Cultures advance much like science. Suddenly a hypothesis is made real. Born is a word used in such moments. It has been said the founders delivered a nation. It has also been said founders are delivered by their mothers.

This essay focuses on the cannabinoid receptor's role in reproduction by highlighting a bit of research for each receptor. We've also taken the liberty of pairing Jay, Hamilton and Madison with a receptor.

# CB1

### *John Jay, revolutionary and First Chief Justice of the US Supreme Court*

The effect of ovarian hormones on the synthesis of anandamide depends on different physiological conditions, oestrous cycle and early pregnancy, and on the presence of the activated blastocyst. Thus, ovarian hormones, as signals that emanate from the mother, operate in conjunction with the blastocyst intrinsic programme, regulating the synthesis of anandamide in a specific manner during crucial reproductive events that may compromise pregnancy outcome.

*Reproductive Biomedicine 2009*

Cannabis is the primary focus of the war on drugs. Nearly half of all US drug arrests are for cannabis. That translates into 800,000 citizens arrested by law enforcement for modulating their receptors. The federal government has many constitutional powers, as *Publius 1787-88* detailed in *The Federalist Papers*. Policing biological receptors involved in all aspects of human life is not one of the powers enumerated.

# CB2
## *Alexander Hamilton, revolutionary and First Secretary of the US Treasury*

This review will focus on the involvement of type-2 cannabinoid (CB2) receptors in reproductive biology, covering both the male and female sides. It will also discuss the potential relevance of the immunological activity of CB2 at the maternal/foetal interface, as well as the distinctiveness of CB2 versus type-1 cannabinoid (CB1) receptors that might be exploited for a receptor subtype-specific regulation of fertility. In this context, the different signalling pathways triggered by CB1 and CB2 (especially those controlling the intracellular tone of nitric oxide), the different activation of CB1 and CB2 by endogenous agonists (like anandamide and 2-arachidonoylglycerol) and the different localization of CB1 and CB2 within membrane subdomains, termed "lipid rafts," will be discussed. It is hoped that CB2-dependent endocannabinoid signalling might become a useful target for correcting infertility, in both men and women.

*British Journal of Pharmacology 2008*

The drug war allows authorities to monitor our past cannabis use and prevent future use. If herbal cannabis use climbs, prohibitionists need more money for the drug war. If use falls, they need more money to keep up the fight. That is a politically cynical Catch-22 masquerading as social policy.

---

# CB3
## *James Madison, revolutionary and POTUS 4*

Together with the endogenous cannabinoids (ECs) and the respective metabolizing-enzymes, the cannabinoid receptors complete the endocannabinoid system (ECS). Two cannabinoid receptors have been described so far, CB1 and CB2, though a third has been suggested, CB3. In order to investigate the expression of GPR55, referred as **the novel cannabinoid receptor 3 (CB3)**, in the uterine maternal tissues during normal pregnancy we analyzed its expression by Q-PCR, Western blot and immunohistochemistry during fetoplacental period. **GPR55** was found in uterine natural killer (uNK) cells pointing to an involvement in the immunological reactions that occur during pregnancy. The prominent expression of **GPR55** in decidual cells suggests a role in mediating cannabinoid signaling during fetoplacental development. The data presented here may clarify the role of GPR55 in fetoplacental development and highlights the presence of **a new target for cannabinoid signaling during pregnancy**.

*Placenta 2011*

---

Despite 70 years of cannabis prohibition, we can still note that cannabis has improved human lives more substantially than cannabis laws have repressed human freedom – and we can take that to be a good sign of things to come. Despite the best efforts of prohibitionists, the CS is going to win this war. No surprise though – like the CS, this plant is resilient in ways we don't even comprehend yet.

*Publius*
(2011)

**Search terms**
GPR55; cannabinoid receptors; CS and reproduction, pregnancy and blastocyst; Publius 1787-88; John Jay; Alexander Hamilton; James Madison.

**Research and selected readings**
2011: B Fonseca, et al, *Modulation of the novel cannabinoid receptor – GPR55 – during rat fetoplacental development*, Placenta, June 2011:32(6):462-9.

2011: J Kargl, et al, The *GPCR – associated sorting protein 1 regulates ligand-induced downregulation of GPR55*, British Journal of Pharmacology, 30 June 2011 [Epub].

2010: R Pertwee, et al, *International Union of Basic and Clinical Pharmacology. LXXIX. Cannabinoid receptors and their ligands: beyond CB1 and CB2,* Pharmacological Review, December 2010:62(4):588-631.

2010: H Patsos, et al, *The endogenous cannabinoid, anandamide, induces COX-2-dependent cell death in apoptosis-resistant colon cancer cells,* International Journal of Oncology, July 2010:37(1):187-93.

2010: J Nones, et al, *Cannabinoids modulate cell survival in embryoid bodies*, Cell Biology International, March 2010:34(4):399-408.

2009: A Kapur, et al, *Atypical responsiveness of the orphan receptor GPR55 to cannabinoid ligands*, Biological Chemistry, October 2009:284(43):29817-27.

2009: F Borrelli and A Izzo, *Role of acylethanolamides in the gastrointestinal tract with special reference to food intake and energy balance*, Best Practice & Research: Clinical Endocrinology & Metabolism, February 2009:23(1):33-49.

2009: M Ribeiro, et al, *17beta-oestradiol and progesterone regulate anandamide synthesis in the rat uterus*, Reproductive Biomedicine, February 2009:18(2):209-18.

2008: O Habayeb, et al, *Expression of the endocannabinoid system in human first trimester placenta and its role in trophoblast proliferation*, Endocrinology, October 2008:149(10):5052-60.

2008: M Maccarrone, *CB2 receptors in reproduction*, British Journal of Pharmacology, January 2008:153(2):189-98.

2007: E Ryberg, et al, *The orphan receptor GPR55 is a novel cannabinoid receptor*, British Journal of Pharmacology, December 2007:152(7):1092-101.

2007: A Greenhough, et al, *The cannabinoid delta-9-tetrahydrocannabinol inhibits RAS-MAPK and PI3K-AKT survival signaling and induces BAD-mediated apoptosis in colorectal cancer cells*, International Journal of Cancer, November 2007:121(10):2172-80.

2006: T Esch, et al, *Endocannabinoids as molecular instruments of health promotion [article in German]*, Medizinische Monatsschrift Pharmazeuten, November 2006:29(11):397-403.

#34

## "The Tomato Effect"

*Once thought to be poison, Americans now consume more*
*than 70 pounds per person of processed tomatoes annually.*

I have always been successful at growing cherry and grape tomato plants on my modest, urban back porch. This year I branched out and planted red leaf lettuce, chives, parsley, basil and rosemary. Picking and eating such produce rekindled my gardening muse. With my joy further rooted, I was prompted to grow even more edibles instead of my usual array of annual flowers.

While reading up on planting and harvesting I came across the term "**The Tomato Effect**." Not being familiar with this phrase I was quite surprised to discover what it meant. It was coined in medicine to mean **the rejection of effective medical treatments because they conflict with currently accepted medical theories**.

The phrase comes from a time when lots of people had been taught to fear tomatoes as poisonous. Though Europeans had been eating tomatoes for centuries, most Americans avoided consuming the easy-to-grow staple of the home garden until about 1820. People who spread the killer-tomato myth probably thought they were doing their best to ensure the safety of their families. In the end, truth won out.

Now, far from poison, Americans see tomatoes as a health food, loaded with Vitamin-C and such essentials as lycopene, an entouraging phyto-chemical used by every organ in the human body. Let's see how the tomato rose from being vilified to the one vegetable that most parents are relieved to know their kids will always eat (as long as it's crushed and spread on pizza dough).

The plant's genetic evidence says it hails from South America and the highlands of Peru. In Europe, one of the earliest English cultivators was John Gerard, a barber-surgeon, who published *Gerard's Herbal* in 1597. Gerard knew that the tomato was eaten in both Spain and Italy, but he still thought it poisonous. His views were influential in Britain and its North American colonies, where most considered the tomato unfit for eating. Many also thought the tomato was an aphrodisiac, thus making it a danger both to physical and spiritual health. The tomatoes acceptance as food was very slow and lasted more than a hundred years. By the mid-1700s though, tomatoes were becoming common in Britain.

The earliest reference to tomatoes being grown in British North America is from 1710, when herbalist William Salmon reported seeing them in today's South Carolina. By the mid-18th century, they were cultivated on some Carolina plantations and probably in other parts of the South as well. In general, they were grown more as ornamental plants than as food. People like Thomas Jefferson, who ate tomatoes in Paris and sent some seeds home, knew the tomato was edible: most Americans thought otherwise.

The most famous legend regarding *The Tomato Effect* concerns a Colonel Robert G. Johnson. At noon on September 26, 1820, Johnson proclaimed he would put to rest any doubt regarding the tomatoes safety by eating a basket of them in front of the Salem Courthouse in New Jersey. A crowd of more than 2,000 gathered to watch the Colonel die after eating the poisonous fruit: the crowd was shocked when he lived. By 1900, tomato consumption in the United States was slowly increasing despite the killer-tomato myth living on in Britain and America, keeping the old stigma in place.

So what do *The Tomato Effect* and *The Cannabis Effect* have in common? The cannabis plant, prior to its federal prohibition, played an important role in many cultural aspects, to include agriculture, industry, military and medicine. Seven decades of research have proven that cannabinoids are biological and that the CS is fundamental to life. That makes the war on cannabinoids seem ridiculous – so much so that the story of cannabis can no longer be told without discussing *The Cannabis Effect*. All we need now is our Colonel Johnson moment … any volunteers?

For those of you who have taken a bite or smoke of the evil weed and lived, I want to remind you of the importance of living in a free society – a society where use does not mean abuse. When a critical mass is achieved, step-by-step, book-by-book, and conversation-by-conversation, truth takes on a life of its own. The new truth begins to look like something others can live with. Change begins to look appealing, and perhaps even better. We are at that point. Let the science lead, as international and domestic cannabinoid research is finally catching up with what many have known for decades. A war against the CS is a war against being healthy.

Perhaps more than any other medicine found in nature, the cannabis plant has helped humans become human. Now that Americans in many states are growing legal cannabis alongside tomatoes warms my heart. Like many other gardeners, I and my muse look forward to the harvest – especially the homegrown and healthy kind.

*Publius*
*(2011)*


### Search terms
*The Tomato Effect*; lycopene and carotenoid activity; fruit vs. vegetable, *US Supreme Court, Nix vs. Hedden (1893)*.


### Research and selected readings
2010: D Mostofsky, *Social science, behavioural medicine, and the tomato effect*, Evaluation in Clinical Practice, 25 October 2010 [Epub].

2010: J Gertsch, et al, *Phytocannabinoids beyond the Cannabis plant – do they exist?* British Journal of Pharmacology, June 2010:160(3):523-9.

2010: E Scotter, et al, *The endocannabinoid system as a target for the treatment of neurodegenerative disease*, British Journal of Pharmacology, June 2010:160(3):480-98.

2010: L De Petrocellis and V Di Marzo, *Non-CB1, non-CB2 receptors for endocannabinoids, plant cannabinoids, and synthetic cannabimimetics: focus on G-protein-coupled receptors and transient receptor potential channels*, Neuroimmune Pharmacology, March 2010:5(1):103-21.

2010: N Jones, et al, *Cannabidiol displays antiepileptiform and antiseizure properties in vitro and in vivo*, Pharmacology and Experimental Therapeutics, February 2010:332(2):569-77.

1990: A Smith, *The making of the legend of Robert Gibbon Johnson and the tomato*, New Jersey Historical Society, Winter 1990:108:59-74.

1984: R Podell, *The 'tomato effect' in clinical nutrition: new treatments languishing on the vine?* Postgraduate Medicine, December 1984:76(8): 49-52, 61-3, 65.

1984: JS Goodwin and JM Goodwin, *The tomato effect. Rejection of highly efficacious therapies*, American Medical Association, May 1984:251(18):2387-90.

1965: A Crosby, *America, Russia, hemp and Napoleon: American trade with Russia and the Baltic 1783-1812*, Ohio State University Press, Columbus OH.

#35

# The thrifty ways of nature

*Then God said, "Let the land produce vegetation: seed-bearing plants and trees on the land that bear fruit with seed in it, according to their various kinds." And it was so.*

*Genesis 1:11*

In this essay we'd like to mention a few interesting cannabinoid connections that we didn't get to cover in more detail. The subtitle for *The Cannabis Papers* points to our emphasis as a "guidebook." We realized early on that we were ignorant about cannabinoids. Then we realized pretty much everyone was. Then we realized that was no longer a problem in the 21$^{st}$ century – we had PubMed, for example. Time was the problem, mainly the lack thereof. So we created this guidebook for ourselves as much as for you.

*A guidebook is designed for the misguided.* It helps you get to your destination – in this case, an understanding of cannabinoids. Along the way we saw this natural pattern: ***cannabinoid modulation is thrifty***. To explain this pattern we will use the three headings Hempy, Healthy and Happy.

**Hempy**

There is little variance in the many translations of Genesis 1:11. The point is always the same: a Creator made seeds, not us. Cannabis is a

***seed-bearing plant*** and has been for millions of years. It is organic and a part of nature, just like us. To make it this far, the plant developed a thrifty persona. It needs little. It grows in ditches and other inhospitable places. Thrift is part of its nature. Thrift is how it survived.

Herbal and synthetic cannabinoids have a simple structure that facilitates stability and use. They store well and are easily metabolized. Thrift is found in the molecular structure of fatty acids and cannabinoids. Both are formed by a specific number of carbon, hydrogen and oxygen atoms connected together. The thriftiness of the CS is exhibited in its ability to work with many different chemicals. For example, fatty acids are a vital source of fuel. When metabolized they produce large quantities of ***adenosine triphosphate (ATP)*** – known as the ***"molecular unit of currency."*** Here are three omega fats that produce ATP. We have listed their molecular formulas and corresponding acids:

| | | |
|---|---|---|
| Omega-3 | $C^{18}H^{30}O^2$ | Linolenic, DHA, EPA |
| Omega-6 | $C^{20}H^{30}O^2$ | Arachidonic |
| Omega-9 | $C^{18}H^{34}O^2$ | Oleic, Stearic |

This shows three fatty acids with slightly different molecular formulas. Now look at these three cannabinoids, two herbal and one synthetic, with the ***same*** molecular formula:

| | |
|---|---|
| Delta-9 THC | $C^{21}H^{30}O^2$ |
| Cannabidiol | $C^{21}H^{30}O^2$ |
| Marinol | $C^{21}H^{30}O^2$ |

Then add this interesting intricacy:

**Progesterone** is $C^{21}H^{30}O^2$

So one could ask – ***You mean to tell me the most notorious cannabinoid of them all, the one they don't allow anywhere, not***

***even in Hempmilk, even though it kills cancer, you're trying to tell me that molecule looks exactly like the hormone Progesterone?***

Yeah, it does. That is an example of thrift in nature, where the same good works differently in different life forms. There's also another thrifty thing nature is good at – **mimicry**, which is the behavior of copying another life form. Mimicry is fundamental to the connections we have to other humans; just watch a mother, father and child for a few interactions and you'll witness mimicry.

Our friends at Cayman Chemical have also noted this behavior. In the 2011 research essay *Cannabinoid Signaling: The Original Retrograde Signaling Pathway*, they have a section heading titled **CB Mimetics and Related Compounds**. Here's what they have in mind. Examine these three endocannabinoids and you'll notice they don't look that much alike:

| | |
|---|---|
| Anandamide | $C^{22}H^{37}NO^2$ |
| 2-AG | $C^{23}H^{38}O^4$ |
| Oleamide | $C^{18}H^{35}NO$ |

All three *endos* vary slightly yet work together in modulation of the CS. Anandamide and oleamide need a nitrogen atom to exist, whereas 2-AG doesn't. All three have oxygen atoms, yet at varying numbers. Oleamide stands out for being the only cannabinoid listed in this section that doesn't have at least two oxygen atoms.

It appears that nature designed the CS to be thrifty, a quality needed to modulate a lifetime of experiences.


**Healthy**

It's hard to place a value on a good night's sleep, some psychic space for the mind to unwind, or the ability to eat without nausea. Difficult to understand a woman's post-partum depression or a soldier's post-traumatic stress disorder. Getting back to healthy is not always easy. A person in pain or suffering or looking to modulate their consciousness deserves the right to cannabinoid supplements. They shouldn't be illegal. Well, not all of them are.

**The Black Hole Appetite Enhancement Formula** is a legal supplement. Its label proudly proclaims a love for *"Cannabinomimetic Alkylamides."* Their product guide delights in Black Hole's ability to activate *both* cannabinoid receptors:

> ***The next step was to look for herbs that contained these alkylamides that mimic the structure of cannabinoids.*** The two herbs that showed the greatest promise were Echinacea Purpurea and Spilanthes Acmella. Both of these herbs contain many different alkylamides, but ***recent clinical information has suggested that there are 3 in particular that have a high affinity for binding to both the CB1 and CB2 receptors.*** Dodeca-2E,4E,8Z,10Z/E-tetraenoic acid isobutylamide and dodeca-2E,4E-dienoic acid isobutylamide from the Echinacea herb and undeca-2E,7Z,9E-trienoic acid isobutylamide from the Spilanthes herb, found in a precise blend in Black Hole, could be ***used to mimic the herbal cannabinoids, and more importantly, the endogenous cannabinoids found in the human body, including anandamide. Not only does the clinical information suggest that they can mimic them, but they can even bind to the receptors for a longer period of time than can the other two types.***

Legal binding to *"both the CB1 and CB2 receptors"* at an online supplement store near you! Here we've been portraying cannabinoid prohibition as absolute. That is no longer true. **The Black Hole Appetite Enhancement Formula** has beaten prohibition! It is legally attempting to activate the CS for health effects. That makes it an interesting sign. It shows instability in the logic of prohibition. It also shows the logic of cannabinoids is winning.

Winning isn't victory though: for that we need a *thrifty* peace – one recognizing a citizen's right to herbal cannabinoid supplementation. We'll have a better name as well, something like **The Green Plant Appetite Enhancement Formula**.


## Happy

In discussions while writing this book, some of us talked at length about how today's *"always on the go"* culture makes contentment nearly impossible. One finds that they are always doing, going and looking for more no matter how much doing, going and looking they've already done. The CS, by design, allows us the ability to step outside the world of constant movement and notice a kind of happiness in the present. One writer mentioned how you can reduce the constant impulse to go out (just for the sake of going out) with cannabinoid supplementation.

Well-known cannabinoids have a more in-depth research database to draw on. The less-known cannabinoids are now drawing the attention of researchers. Here are three to keep track of:

| | |
|---|---|
| Cannabigerol | $C^{21}H^{32}O^2$ |
| Cannabichromene | $C^{21}H^{30}O^2$ |
| Tetrahydrocannabivarin | $C^{19}H^{26}O^2$ |

Cannabigerol (CBG) is found in plants with little THC. This would be your common "ditch weed" that grows throughout America. THC's leading role in cannabinoid history has also allowed it to dominate research. CBG is drawing more attention because of its dynamic receptor activity. It has strong activity at *adrenergic receptors*, moderate modulation of *serotonin 5HT-1 receptors*, and low affinity for *CB1*. Cannabigerol also activates *CB2 receptors*; to what strength and action is still being researched.

Cannabichromene (CBC) also has the seemingly ever-present molecular formula of $C^{21}H^{30}O^2$. Its role in the CS was thought to be as an entourager. CBC has anti-inflammatory effects that improve with the addition of THC. Its future is likely to change soon. One issue in researching CBC has been its receptor activity. It didn't seem to activate CB1 or CB2. With the recent discovery of the CB3 receptor, our understanding of the activity of this cannabinoid is likely to improve.

Tetrahydrocannabivarin (THCV) is considered special for its "high" content: some varieties of cannabis are more than 50% THCV. It is a CS antagonist for CB1 receptors and is in clinical trials at GW Pharmaceuticals as a treatment for type 2 diabetes.

Thrifty implies economical and frugal, industrious and thriving, and even prosperous. *The word also describes a thriving plant growing vigorously.* That's definitely our weed, always growing with vigor.

*Publius*
*(2011)*


### Search terms
Genesis 1:11; fatty acids *arachidonic* (ARA), *docosahexaenoic* (DHA), *eicosapentaenoic* (EPA), *linolenic, oleic,* and *stearic*; ATP; cannabigerol; cannabichromene; tetrahydrocannabivarin; cannabinoid mimetics; DHA/EPA Omega-3 Institute.


### Research and selected readings
2011: T Brock, *Cannabinoid signaling: the original retrograde signaling pathway*, Cayman Chemical online.

2011: M Pascoe, et al, *What you eat is what you are – a role for polyunsaturated fatty acids in neuroinflammation induced depression?* Clinical Nutrition, 27 May 2011 [Epub].

2010: T Esch and G Stefano, *The neurobiology of stress management*, Neuro Endocrinology Letters, 2010:31(1):19-39.

2010: L De Petrocellis, et al, *Effects of cannabinoids and cannabinoid-enriched cannabis extracts on TRP channels and endocannabinoid metabolic enzymes*, British Journal of Pharmacology, 22 December 2010 [Epub].

2010: J Hoggatt and M Pelus, *Eicosanoid regulation of hematopoiesis and hematopoietic stem and progenitor trafficking*, Leukemia, December 2010:24(12):1993-2002.

2010: A Lichtman, et al, *Endocannabinoid overload*, Molecular Pharmacology, December 2010:78(6):993-5.

2010: G DeLong, et al, *Pharmacological evaluation of the natural constituent of cannabis sativa, cannabichromene and its modulation by delta-9-tetrahydrocannabinol*, Drug and Alcohol Dependence, November 2010:112(1-2):126-33.

2010: W Marrs, et al, *The serine hydrolase ABHD6 controls the accumulation and efficacy of 2-AG at cannabinoid receptors*, Nature Neuroscience, August 2010:13(8):951-7.

2010: A El-Alfy, et al, *Antidepressant-like effect of delta9-tetrahydrocannabinol and other cannabinoids isolated from cannabis sativa L,* Pharmacology, Biochemistry, and Behavior, June 2010:95(4):434-42.

2010: H Taylor, et al, *Histomorphometric evaluation of cannabinoid receptor and anandamide modulating enzyme expression in the human endometrium through the menstrual cycle*, Histochemistry and Cell Biology, May 2010:133(5):557-65.

2010: M Cascio, et al, *Evidence that the plant cannabinoid cannabigerol is a highly potent alpha2-adrenoceptor agonist and moderately potent 5HT1A antagonist*, British Journal of Pharmacology, January 2010:159(1):129-41.

2008: L De Petrocellis, et al, *Plant-derived cannabinoids modulate the activity of transient receptor potential channels of ankyrin type-1 and melastatin type-8*, Pharmacology and Experimental Therapeutics, June 2008:325(3):1007-15.

2007: R Mangieri and D Piomelli, *Enhancement of endocannabinoid signaling and the pharmacotherapy of depression*, Pharmacological Research, November 2007:56(5):360-6.

2005: J Shoemaker, et al, *The endocannabinoid noladin ether acts as a full agonist at human CB2 receptors*, Pharmacological and Experimental Therapeutics, August 2005:314(2):868-75.

2004: L Walter, et al, *ATP induces a rapid and pronounced increase in 2-arachidonoylglycerol production by astrocytes, a response limited by monoacylglycerol lipase*, Neuroscience, September 2004:24(37):8068-74.

#36

# Weed appreciation

*What is a weed? A plant whose virtues have not yet been discovered.*

*Ralph Waldo Emerson*

Chickens are a big part of America's diet. We noted in essay *#15* the relationship between egg-bearing animals can be traced back to 550 million years ago.

There's been an update that begins to unfold the evolution of a cousin of mammals, the chicken. Fowl lay eggs and mammals give birth. It has recently been reported we have something else in common with the egg-layers, in particular, the chicken. Chickens have CB1 receptors. Look at this transcendent title: *The localization and physiological effects of cannabinoid receptor 1 in the brain stem auditory system of the chick.* No joke: chickens use cannabinoids.

Which brings us to weeds, or more precisely, ***Weed***.

Referring to cannabis as a weed is not slang. As Emerson noted and we've been discussing, cannabis is a plant whose virtues are not fully understood.

Walt Whitman, a transcendental associate of Emerson's, wrote "Poem of The Body" in *Leaves of Grass* (1856). Here is an excerpt on … well lots of things:

*The female contains all qualities, and tempers them – she is in her place, she moves with perfect balance, she is all things duly veiled,*

*She is both passive and active – she is to conceive daughters as well as sons, and sons as well as daughters.*

*As I see my soul reflected in nature, as I see through a mist one with inexpressible completeness and beauty — see the bent head and arms folded over the breast, the female I see,*

*I see the bearer of the great fruit which is immortality— the good thereof is not tasted by roués, and never can be.*

*The male is not less the soul, nor more—he too is in his place,*

*He too is all qualities, he is action and power, the flush of the known universe is in him,*

*Scorn becomes him well, and appetite and defiance become him well,*

*The fiercest largest passions, **bliss** that is utmost, sorrow that is utmost, become him well —*

*Life, Liberty and the Pursuit of Happiness* frame this guidebook. It kept us on task. It allowed us to quote a Creator and honor seeds and eggs, to find liberty in the midst of war, and to pursue happiness.

Cannabis is a special kind of commodity. In modulating the CS it helps with sound sleep, refreshing reflections, and enhanced appetite. Cannabis helps us transcend momentary negativity with a fresh perspective. These simple every day moments are pathways on the pursuit of happiness.

*Publius*
*(2011)*

### Search terms
Ralph Waldo Emerson; Walt Whitman; *Leaves of Grass*; bliss.

### Research and selected readings
2011: A Howlett, et al, *Endocannabinoid tone versus constitutive activity of cannabinoid receptors*, British Journal of Pharmacology, August 2011:163(7):1329-43.

2011: M Rock, et al, *Interaction between non-psychotropic cannabinoids in marihuana: effect of cannabigerol (CBG) on the anti-nausea or anti-emetic effects of cannabidiol (CBD) in rats and shrews*, Psychopharmacology (Berl), June 2011:215(3):505-12.

2011: T Stincic and R Hyson, *The localization and physiological effects of cannabinoid receptor 1 in the brain stem auditory system of the chick*, Neuroscience, 7 June 2011 [Epub].

2011: M Sordelli, et al, *The effect of anandamide on uterine nitric oxide synthase activity depends on the presence of the blastocyst*, PLoS One, April 2011:6(4):e18368.

2010: C Streeter, et al, *Effects of yoga versus walking on mood, anxiety and brain GABA levels: a randomized controlled MRS study*, Alternative and Complementary Medicine, November 2010:16(11):1145-52.

2009: R Nyilas, et al, *Molecular architecture of endocannabinoid signaling at nociceptive synapses mediating analgesia*, European Journal of Neuroscience, May 2009:29(10):1964-78.

2001: D Zhou and Z Song, *CB1 cannabinoid receptor-mediated neurite remodeling in mouse neuroblastoma N1E-115 cells,* Neuroscience Research, August 2001:65(4):346-53.

1997: A Schatz, et al, *Cannabinoid receptors CB1 and CB2: a characterization of expression and adenylate cyclase modulation within the immune system,* Toxicology and Applied Pharmacology, February 1997:142(2):278-87.

1995: S Galieque, et al, *Expression of central and peripheral cannabinoid receptors in human immune tissues and leukocyte subpopulations,* European Journal of Biochemistry, August 1995:232(1):54-61.

1993: M Bouaboula, et al, *Cannabinoid-receptor expression in human leukocytes,* European Journal of Biochemistry, May 1993:214(1):173-80.

1991: R Mechoulam, et al, *A random walk through a cannabis field,* Pharmacology, Biochemistry, and Behavior, November 1991:40(3):461-4.

―――――――     ―――――――     ―――――――

*Good listeners try to understand thoroughly what the other is saying. In the end they may disagree sharply, but before they disagree, they want to know exactly what it is.*

*Kenneth A. Wells inspired*

―――――――  ―――――――     ―――――――

*Potscript ~*

# Cannabinoids are nature's healthcare plan

> *Humans, and all animals, make and use internally*
> *produced cannabis-like products (endocannabinoids)*
> *as part of the evolutionary harm reduction program.*

2005 Harm Reduction Journal

An Illinois State Senator once remarked she was having a hard time considering "marijuana" as medicine. Of course she couldn't. She couldn't get past the word marijuana and all of its meanings next to the word medical. They don't go together in word flow, especially since one has a million negative images and the other is generally positive.

*Harm reduction – the cannabis paradox* was the title for the journal article quoted above. After reading this book, you've probably noticed how much things keep changing in this war. One month there is speculation of a CB3 receptor: the next month there's new research from the white-coats saying they've found the receptor. It's been like that for years now.

The paradox mentioned is found in our politics not our cannabinoids. This is one of the evolutions in cannabis thinking. Cannabis has gone from good to bad, to harm reducer, to good and now great. That's the power of science and it's not a moderate approach. Neither is the right to be let alone, to self-medicate or to

209

pursue happiness. No one would call Life and Liberty moderate concepts either.

What happens next? That's a common question at the end of a political book. People want to know what to do, thinking it can all change in one quick burst of energy.

No. This is a political action. We have to be better informed. We have to know ourselves and our opposition. We have to know what is at risk. The clearest move is an action against Nixon's law, the Controlled Substances Act. **Repeal it**. Like Nixon, you can't reform something corrupt – **the CSA must go**.

Okay, that's the objective. The war on cannabis will not end until the CSA is repealed and replaced by a law respecting nature, i.e. the CS. In some funny way, eliminating the prohibition of cannabis is a victory for science and against ignorance. It surprised us. We began thinking all we had to do was explain the evils of the war and people would listen. We thought things would change if they only knew that cannabis relieves the pain of glaucoma and remyelinates nerve damage, or that minorities were being arrested disproportionately for it. We thought we would just let the world know and then reason would win out.

Well, it's more complicated than just the facts. That's when it crosses over into politics.

*We the People* possess a great opportunity: by holding the patent on the neuroprotective qualities of cannabinoids, we have prohibition right where we want it. We have an opportunity for cannabis clarity. To an advocate for *Life, Liberty and the Pursuit of Happiness*, the role of cannabinoids is unambiguous. The ideas formed by the word "Marijuana" have historically ranged from madness to hilarity.

Today the theory that cannabis is a harm reduction agent is accepted by the white-coats and activists – anyone who begins to understand the role of the CS in health. The 2005 abstract quoted at the opening of this essay closed with this summary:

> ***More specifically, endocannabinoids homeostatically regulate all body systems (cardiovascular, digestive,***

*endocrine, excretory, immune, nervous, musculo-skeletal, reproductive). Therefore, the health of each individual is dependent on this system working appropriately.*

Great change is challenging. Once individuals start acknowledging and using the evidence about cannabinoids, political groups will form. With such a new beginning one opens the pathway of science. The inscrutable path, our present path of the omnipotent CSA and its reliance on discredited science, is dogma. A cannabinoider avoids dogma because it is based on belief.

Faith is an act of the mind and body. It is biological. Politics built on dogma traditionally suffer from a lack of adaptability. In the future, which officially begins now, marijuana dogma is being replaced and defeated by cannabinoid science. – Good thing we're ready for it.

*Publius*
*(2011)*

### Search terms
Homeostasis of endocannabinoids and the cardiovascular, digestive, endocrine, excretory, immune, nervous, musculo-skeletal and reproductive systems; cannabinoids and osteoporosis.

### Research and selected readings
2011: Y Sun, et al, *Target-dependent control of synaptic inhibition by endocannabinoids in the thalamus*, Neuroscience, June 2011:31(25):9222-30.

2011: T Yoshida, et al, *Unique inhibitory synapse with particularly rich endocannabinoid signaling machinery on pyramidal neurons in basal amygdaloid nucleus*, Proceedings of the National Academy of Sciences USA, February 2011:108(7):3059-64.

2010: S Wolf, et al, *Cannabinoid receptor CB1 mediates baseline and activity-induced survival of new neurons in adult hippocampal neurogenesis*, Cell Communication and Signaling, June 2010:8:12.

2009: I Bab, et al, *Cannabinoids and the skeleton: from marijuana to reversal of bone loss*, Annals of Medicine, 2009:41(8):560-7.

2009: J Galligan, *Cannabinoid signaling in the enteric nervous system*, Neurogastroenterology and Motility, September 2009:21(9):899-902.

2009: M Roloff and S Thayer, *Modulation of excitatory synaptic transmission by Delta 9-tetrahydrocannabinol switches from agonist to antagonist depending on firing-rate*, Molecular Pharmacology, April 2009:75(4):892-900.

2005: R Melamede, *Harm reduction – the cannabis paradox*, Harm Reduction Journal, September 2005:2:17.

## ***Bonus video links ~ and thank you!***

*BBC special ~ Cannabinoid receptors in the human body*

*Film ~ What if cannabis cured cancer?*

*Robert Randall ~ First US medical cannabis patient*

*William Courtney ~ juicing cannabis and Cannabis International*

*Ester Fride ~ Lab mouse (on YouTube)*

*The Human Revolution's "Tree of Life"*

*Lindy's "No Knock Raid"*

*Cab Calloway's "Reefer Man"*

*Cab Calloway's "Smoking Reefers" (unreleased/banned)*

*Harlem Hamfats' "Weed Smoker's Dream"*

*Lil's Hot Shots with Louis Armstrong ~ "Drop That Sack"*

*Crucial Conflict's "Hay"*

*President Obama talking about smoking reefer*

*Michael Backes' medical cannabis primer*

*Film ~ Charles Shaw's Exile Nation*

*Film ~ Ron Mann's Grass*

# Index

ABILIFY, 88-91
Abrams, Donald, 115
Acetaminophen (see Paracetamol), 157-62
Acetylcholine, 165-6
Action potentials, 169-74
Adams, Roger, 19-22, 115
Adipocytes, 131-2, 154
Adipose tissue (see fat), 102, 104, 130-3
Agonist, 26, 54, 123, 165, 167, 189, 203-4, 212
Alcohol (ethanol), 16-7, 20, 53, 70, 89-92, 94, 97, 107-8, 117-8, 132, 138, 157, 203; alcoholism, 16-7, 117-21, 138; driving, 90-2; crime, 129; prohibition, 70, 118-9, 129, 155; withdrawal, 117-9, 120; violence, 119
Alexander, Michelle, 177-81
Alzheimer's, 53-4, 112-4
Americans for Safe Access (ASA), 35
AMPA receptor, 172, 174
Amygdala, 114, 120, 145, 169-75, 181
Analgesia, 79, 161, 207
Anandamide (AEA), 10-2, 17, 20-1, 26, 32, 48, 61, 65, 73, 78, 82-5, 104, 118, 131, 138, 142, 144-5, 150, 161, 165, 167, 184-6, 188-92, 199-200, 203, 207
Antagonist, 96, 123, 165, 202-3, 212
Antidepressants, 46, 107, 150
Apoptosis, 23-5, 62, 64, 115, 132, 191-2
Arachidonic acid (ARA, Omega-6), 103-4, 158, 162, 198, 202
Araque, Alfonso, 25-6
Arevalo-Martin, Angel, 42-3, 126-7
Armstrong, Louis, 61-4, 102, 147, 213
Astrocytes, 23-6, 204
ATP, 198, 202, 204

Basavarajappa, Balapal, 54, 120, 138
Berg, Chris, 89
Bisogno, Tiziana, 49, 54, 154
Black Sabbath, 184-5
Blastocyst, 10-2, 188, 191, 207
Bliss, 20, 61, 64, 141-4, 206-7

Lipogenesis, 131-2
Lycopene, 193, 195

Maccarrone, Mauro, 85, 149-50, 186, 192
Madison, James (see POTUS 4), xiii, 141, 187, 190-1
Maejima, Takashi, 115, 127
Magbie, Jonathan, 41-3, 179
Mammalian, xii, 4, 6, 12, 82, 100, 103, 184, 205
Marihuana/Marijuana, xi-xiv, 7, 12, 14, 19-20, 22, 30, 32, 34-5, 39, 42, 51-3, 59, 65, 70-3, 92, 115, 126, 131-2, 136-8, 155, 167, 182, 186, 209-12
Marihuana Tax Act (1937), 51, 69-70
Marinol (Dronabinol), 4-6, 88, 107, 118, 143-4, 198
Marty, Alain, 115, 175
Marzo, Vincenzo Di, 7, 32, 36, 49, 54, 132, 138, 154, 174, 186, 196
Melamede, Robert, 181, 209-12
Mechoulam, Raphael, 20-2, 36, 127, 208
Michigan, 35, 137
Mimetics, 199, 200; cannabinomimetics, 162, 196
Modulate, xii-xiii, 4, 10-2, 16-7, 53, 94-5, 130, 138, 142-3, 148, 160, 165, 169, 171-2, 181, 191, 199, 203
Montana, 135-7
Muggles, 61, 64
Multiple Sclerosis (MS), xii, 4-6, 13, 39-43, 127, 131, 161, 173-4
Murillo-Rodriquez, Eric, 48
Musculo-skeletal system, 210-2
Myelin, 24-6, 40-2, 123-7, 210

Nabilone, 6
N-acylethanolamides, 84
National Cancer Institute, 25-6, 62, 64-5
National Institutes of Health (NIH), 25, 46, 64, 123
Nausea, 5, 33-5, 83, 89, 127, 166, 199, 207
Navarrete, Marta, 25-6
Nerves, 3, 23, 40-1, 115, 149
Nervous system, 3, 40, 54, 157, 162, 165, 212
Neurodevelopment, 54
Neurogenesis, 53-4, 97, 212
Neuroprotection, 12, 54, 126-7
Niacinamide, 66
Nicotinamide, 66
Nicotine, 53, 163-5
Nicotine withdrawal, 166
Nicotinic receptors, 166

www.ingramcontent.com/pod-product-compliance
Lightning Source LLC
Chambersburg PA
CBHW051046050726
47592CB00002B/415